It's All In Your Mind

LINDSEY SHARRATT

Copyright © 2015 Lindsey Sharratt

All rights reserved.

ISBN: 1518890962
ISBN-13: 978-1518890963

DEDICATION

This book is dedicated to my aunt, Anita Mash, my first role model.
Also to my grandmother, Sallie Phillips, for sharing her love of learning, French and the piano.

'It's not what you look at that matters, it's what you see.'
~Henry David Thoreau

'There is no psychology; there is only biography and autobiography.'
~Thomas Szasz, The Second Sin: Psychology, 1973

CONTENTS

	Introduction	i
1	Self-Concept Who Am I?	1
2	Biopsychosocial	8
3	Exploring Identity	12
4	Setting Goals	19
5	Reality	30
6	Conditioning	43
7	Stereotyping	53
8	Beliefs, Emotions and Attitudes	62
9	Personality vs. Identity	74
10	Personality	81
11	State Change	95
12	Biology	106
13	Cognition	116
14	Social Environment	131
15	Use of Identities	141
16	Negative Emotions	152
17	Secondary Gain	163

18	Behaviors	169
19	Action Plan	175
20	Conclusion	183

INTRODUCTION

I started writing this book during the first year of my psychology degree. Almost four years later, with a greater understanding of the theory behind me, there are surprisingly few changes to the content. The thought processes that underlie some people being confident, successful and happy, while others spend lives mired in dissatisfaction, frustration and misery, remain the same. In truth, I think there's a greater need for the book than ever. To be able to give people the tools to understand how their self-concept develops, what supports and what hinders them, and how to change that – this was my goal when I first started writing, and it's still my goal now.

So before you start reading, ask yourself - what are you looking to get from this book? Are you unhappy with the way your life has gone? Have you done the things you thought you wanted to do, followed certain paths and directions, and then discovered that you're not content with the end product? Are there things you wanted to do but never did, and now feel something in your life is missing? Or is it simply that you don't have the confidence and direction that you need, the self-belief that will allow you to have the life you believe (or want to believe) you deserve?

If so, you're not alone. I've been there, and I know all about that moment when the realization hits you that you've got stuck on the wrong path.

For me, this moment was a revelation, as I was, in the eyes of all the people around me, successful. I had a lovely family, a wonderful home, an excellent career, good health ... in fact, when I first started to question why I didn't feel completely fulfilled and satisfied with my achievements, friends with whom I tried to discuss this ranged from puzzled to irritated. Most people seemed to think that meeting the world's standards for "doing well in life" should be sufficient for anyone. What else could I possibly want?

The truth is, there is no such thing as a world standard for a fulfilling, satisfying life. Only you know what's right for you, and only you know if you've done the things that you feel you're capable of doing. Sometimes you can realize that there must be more, without being sure of what that is, or how to get it. If that's the case, you can sometimes need a little help to get onto the right road and work out the steps you need to take along it. And that's where this book comes in.

The information in these pages is the product of years of investigation into the things that make people feel, behave and react as they do.

Why is it that two people starting from the same place, doing the same thing, with relatively the same level of skill, can produce such different results?

Why is it that one of those people will exceed all expectations and achieve astonishing levels of success, and the other will fail completely?

Why is that that when you look at two people with very similar lifestyles and achievements, one will be happy and fulfilled, and the other unhappy and dissatisfied?

Why are some people energized and motivated, and some people lethargic and hopeless?

Why do some people seem to go from strength to strength, happy with all that they have achieved to date and eagerly looking forward to the next challenge, while some people never feel complete or fulfilled, no matter how brilliant the things that they manage to do?

The answer, for all of these things and more, seems to come down to one base factor – it's all in your mind. Everything that you think, feel and do is the product of what is already in your head, and in a lot of cases, you won't even know that it's in there. But whether you know it is or not, it will affect you, every single day, in all of your relationships and all of the things that you do.

To say that all of your results in the physical world are a

product of your mental world may seem simplistic, but it's not. The mind is an incredibly sophisticated and complex piece of machinery, which can both provide you with immense help in achieving your goals, and hold you back every time you try to move forward. Very few of us really understand how our minds work, and a lot of the processes that are going on in our heads happen below our own levels of consciousness.

You may think that you're really committed, dedicated and confident, and ready to go out and achieve your dreams. If your mind does not agree with you, you may find that you experience failure, unhappiness and despondency, over and over again.

When I initially started my research into how our minds work to produce the results that we see in our lives, one of the first things that occurred to me was how often people have asked me, how is it that you can do what you do? How is it that when you say you are going to do something, you always manage to do it?

When I started to think about this, my initial response was that I don't let things put me off – and maybe also that it's because I'm a bit stubborn and don't like conceding defeat! However, when I thought about it for a while, I realized it was a lot deeper than that. The main reason is that I always believe that I can do things, and I make sure that I have the information I need to back me up in achieving my goals.

That led to the question, why do I believe that I can do it? And that's when things started to get interesting.

At the time, I was, without having deliberately set out to do it, coaching people I knew, both in work and outside, to try to help them with their issues and to achieve their goals. I'd never thought about what I was doing, or how I did it – coaching was not something I had ever trained in myself or received formally. For as long as I could remember, I was one of those people that others come to when they have problems, and I would try to help. Actually, that's still how I see myself, as a problem-solver who gets satisfaction out of helping others.

It had never occurred to me that I was doing anything out of the ordinary with my life, or achieving things that others could not do if they wanted to. So, I decided that there was obviously a simple answer here to the reason that people aren't always successful in doing the things that they aspire to do in life – and I wanted to work out what it was. I knew that I was just a normal person, doing what I thought of as an ordinary thing – setting goals and hitting them. It had never really occurred to me, even in the process of helping other people, that I was doing something that everyone else did not do every day.

I thought that maybe sometimes people just got a bit stuck, and that if left to themselves they would probably have worked things out anyway – I was just speeding things up a little for them. Now that I'd started to think about this in more detail, I set out to look at what I really felt the root of the problem was – why some people's minds tell them that they can achieve the things they want, and some people's minds tell them that they can't. I felt that if I could find an answer to this simple problem, I could really help people to very quickly make changes in their lives.

Remember that I said I always set out to do the things that I decide to do, and that I'm a bit stubborn? That 'simple' problem turned out to be the most complicated thing that I had ever looked at, and that decision was the start of a lifetime journey that took me through self-development, NLP and a degree in psychology, and is about to take me forward into a PhD. The product of that is this book.

The first thing that I would like to say about 'It's All In Your Mind' is that it's for everyone. You don't need to aspire to be a billionaire, own a FTSE100 company, or to win the Nobel Prize to read this book (although if you do, you will find something in here for you too). You also don't need to have catastrophic, mind-blowing problems. This is a book for everyone who is experiencing frustration or setbacks, or who has a sneaking feeling that they're capable of more than they're doing now – whether that's in career, business, academia, relationships… in fact, it's for anyone who wants some help in shaping their life in the way that they want it to be.

The key to all of these things is understanding your mind. Why you react as you do in certain situations, whether you love or hate challenges, the areas in which you do well or do badly, and your satisfaction with your life accomplishments to date - in fact, pretty much everything that happens to you - is a product of what your mind is doing in the background. For that reason, it's a really good idea to understand the things that are going on in your head; both those things that you're aware of, and the things beneath the surface that impact your thoughts and reactions. If you understand your mind, you can manage it. When you learn to manage it, you can learn to make it work for the things you want, rather than against them.

For instance, when I took my own life as a starting point, I realized that, actually, the people who thought I always achieved everything I set out to do were being too kind to me. It was true that I had, but the things that I set out to do were always those that I thought I could do – which gave me rather an unfair advantage when considering my achievements. It was obvious that I had a clear-cut idea of the things that I was good at, and so I focused my energy in these areas and did well. The things that I didn't feel I was good at, or that I felt were risky, I stayed away from. That led me to consider why I held these beliefs about the areas where I thought I could achieve, and the areas where I felt I could not. Years of study later, I realize that this is all information which I had taken in from an early age, built upon by experience (my own, and that of those around me) and decided subconsciously that this was the 'truth' of life.

Since then, I've deliberately set out to challenge my beliefs in these areas, and have done things that I would never previously have considered. Some of these required a pretty strong mental push to get me started, purely because of my own personal beliefs about doing them. The interesting thing is that most of these were things that I have seen others doing easily and naturally, but some of these same people were those who had been so impressed with my own achievements. Slowly, from speaking to people, observing my own reactions and beliefs and those of others, and studying the science behind the workings of the mind, I began to understand why we think, speak, act and believe as we do – and how much difference it makes to have the knowledge to understand our programming, to be able to take control of our own minds and make them work for our benefit.

The second thing that I would like to say about this book is that it has been an absolute pleasure to write it, and I very much hope that you will get the same amount of pleasure from reading it. Ironically, in my own moment of realization that I was not totally content with my life achievements, one of the things I discovered was the fact that I got much more pleasure and satisfaction out of helping other people than I did from any of the managerial, financial, business-orientated things that I was doing every day. I liked my work, I was good at it, I made a very good living from doing it, but it never gave me the joy and satisfaction that I got from helping others to move their own lives forward. The point at which your development stops is the point at which you decide it stops – you're the one who's driving.

This book, then, aims to offer a path to achieving the things that you really want, by a three stage process. Firstly, it will help you to understand yourself in the present – your dreams and your desires, the things you want that will make you happy and fulfilled, where you are now, and where you would like to be. Next, it will help you to understand the beliefs that you hold about yourself and the world around you, where these beliefs came from, and why you can challenge those that are not helping you and replace them with something more useful to you. It will also help you to understand why you feel as you do about certain things, and why you react in certain ways. Thirdly, with an understanding of these things in mind, you will be able to start planning your steps forward, backed up by more supportive thought processes than you might have had to date.

I believe that everyone has the power to succeed, to achieve happiness, fulfillment and satisfaction with life. I don't believe that we're shown how to do this – mostly because our parents and teachers were not taught this themselves. Once you start to appreciate how much control your mind has over you, once you start to be able to change it to help you gain the life you want, you'll begin to see that things you thought beyond your control are actually within your reach.

The first step, then, is to understand who you are now, and why.

1 SELF-CONCEPT – WHO AM I?

Your self-concept and identity may not be something that you spend a lot of time thinking about. Nevertheless, whether or not you are aware of it, or put a lot of your energy into it, you'll have a picture of yourself in your head, complete with a whole range of associated attributes and characteristics that, combined together, make up the composite picture of the person that you believe yourself to be.

Some people give this very little of their attention. Others dwell on it obsessively, and agonize over how they could be "better". The rest of us fall somewhere in between these two extremes.

All of us have beliefs about the person that we are. These beliefs cover a whole range of different areas which all come together to build the person that we see as 'me'. There are a variety of sources for these beliefs, which we will come onto later in this chapter. However, before we do this, it will help you to understand exactly what beliefs you have.

The best place to start when working towards being the person that you want to be is to have an understanding of the person that you are now. Just like trying to find your way with a map, it's a lot easier to get to your destination if you know where you are starting from.

To do that, try writing down all the beliefs that you have about yourself at the moment.

You will have beliefs about your physical attributes. Some of these are pretty fixed – for example, whether you are tall, medium-height, or short, and your physical age. Some of them can be changed, like the color of your hair or your weight. Some are subjective, for instance whether you feel that you are attractive, unattractive or somewhere in the middle.

You will have beliefs about your characteristics. You may see yourself as shy, stubborn, determined, confident, caring, impatient, selfish, focused, irritable, calm, stressed, overworked … there are a huge array to choose from. Write down all that you believe apply to you. You may find some of them seem to be contradictory, but this is not unusual – write them down anyway. You will understand why this is by the time you get to the end of the book.

Now write down your beliefs about the skills that you have. Are you a good leader? Intelligent? Organized? A great time-keeper? A good athlete? Great at relationship building? Artistic? A good teacher or mentor? Good at empathizing? Good with your hands? Creative? Think of every area where you have a skill.

Some people have said at this point that they don't *have* any skills. When I've discussed this with them further, I can honestly say that I have never found this to be the case. Everyone has a skill in some area. It doesn't matter what this is – all skills are valuable. Take your time to think about everything that you have been good at in your life, every area where you have ever felt satisfaction in your achievements, and write them down.

When you have finished writing down all of your beliefs about your attributes, characteristics and skills, you should have something in the next section which, when you read it, feels like a summary of 'me'. Read it now. Do you feel that it gives you a clear picture of yourself? Does it describe you well? Would the people who know you, recognize you?

"ME"

MY ATTRIBUTES

MY CHARACTERISTICS

_____

MY SKILLS

_____

Read through the section again. What items are missing from it that you would like to add? What do you feel is lacking in your list that, if you had it, would allow you to do the things that you want to do? Is there something fundamental that you feel you are lacking when you look at this summary of yourself? Do you believe that there's something that you don't have and can't get?

If so, the good news is that this summary of 'me' is not set in stone. It's not like a book, where once it goes into print, that's what it contains. This is a *theory* of yourself, and it's built from all of the things that you have experienced in your life. People have the power to change, once they begin to understand why they are as they are now.

We will go into this in much more detail in Chapter 5, but for now, the most important thing is for you to understand that this is what identity is.

Identity it is a theory of ourselves, built up from a number of different sources, which we put together over time.

One of these sources is your self-concept, your 'I', the way that you see yourself. This goes into the theory that you construct about yourself, your identity. So do all the things that you see, hear, and experience, the things that you are told, the things that you pick up about yourself from others. You see yourself, to a great extent, as you believe you are seen. Every experience that you have reinforces one view or another, about yourself, your attributes, your characteristics and your skills. Your brain, which is a great computer, analyses the data that you are giving it and files it away for future reference.

There is a huge benefit to you from being able to do this – it means that you don't have to learn every lesson again from the start. Take the experience of a child trying to touch an open fire. Either the child will feel the heat and pull its fingers away, or an adult will shout at the child not to touch the flames. Either way, the child will learn that it's not a good idea to touch the fire. By the time you're an adult (even by the time that you're an older child) you will have stopped trying to put your hand in the fire. Why? Because you've learned that bad things happen when you do it, and your brain has stored this information. You did not have to get burned to learn this – you made an assumption as your hand got closer to the flames and the heat became uncomfortable, or you trusted the information given to you about it by an adult that it was something you really shouldn't do. Every time you see an open fire, you don't stop to think about what will happen if you touch the flames, and you don't stop to analyze why you think it. Your brain will automatically tell you not to do it, without you needing to think about why you shouldn't.

The downside of this is that your brain may learn some things that are not helpful to you. Remember that we said our identity is a theory of ourselves, which is built from many sources? What if some of those sources were unhelpful? As an adult reading this book, you may say that you can choose to disregard them. This is true, but the problem with that is that your brain will not always be able to distinguish the good information from the bad – and in the same way that you know automatically not to touch a fire, you may not always get the chance to make that choice – not all of our choices are made at a conscious level, and consequently we fall into thought patterns and automatic responses without getting chance to be aware that a decision has even been made.

Say that someone told you, when you were younger, that you were not good at maths, and you believed them. When we are young, we don't have as much ability to reason against the things people tell us as we do when we're older. The chances are, if you respect and admire the person who tells you this, you will believe it. You may even believe it just because they are an adult, and therefore, to a child, an authority figure. Therefore, you will develop a belief that you are not good at maths, in the same way that you developed a belief that putting your hand in the fire will hurt you. The difference, of course, is that fire burning is a fact, and your ability at maths is someone's opinion. The effect, however, is the same. You'll grow up into someone that doesn't put their hands in the fire and doesn't have any confidence in their mathematical ability. That is, unless you challenge your beliefs around maths.

The good news is that it is indeed possible to change these false beliefs, but to do so we need to understand what we are doing, why we are doing it, and how the human mind functions. Giving you back your ability to see the block and make the choice is part of what we'll be doing in this book. In the next chapter, we are going to consider the three building blocks of your experience that build your self-concept.

2 BIOPSYCHOSOCIAL

I set out to make this a book for everyone, and that's what I intend it to be. For that reason, I'm not going to fill it with a lot of psychological terminology. However, there is one word that I really think needs to be understood, because to me it is a key foundation point of understanding why we have become who we are. That word is biopsychosocial. If you never remember another psychology term in your life, I really advise that you remember this one.

So, what does biopsychosocial mean? My friends would tell you that I use that word a lot! It means what it says – biology, psyche (mind) and social conditions. Simply put, you are a product of your own biology, your thought processes and your social environment. These are the conditions in which your self-concept has grown, and they have all influenced its formation. All of those beliefs that you have about yourself which you wrote down in the last chapter developed under the influence of those three things.

In addition to this, they all influence each other – you cannot change one without that change affecting the other two. There is a three-way interaction between the biology of your mind, the way that you think, and the environment that surrounds you.

Let me give an analogy to try to explain this. We can use a computer to illustrate it. The computer's hardware would be the biology – the physical components. The computer's software, its operating system and applications, would be the psyche – the processes by which the computer works. The office in which the computer was sitting would be the social environment.

If the computer's hardware is slow or faulty, the operating system and applications won't be able to work correctly, even if they are properly installed. You would need to fix and repair the hardware before the software could function properly. If the software was corrupt, then however good the computer's hardware was, then it would not work efficiently. And if the computer was sitting in a cold, damp office, then regardless of how good the hardware and software were, then it would stop working correctly.

Ensuring that the computer's hardware was fully functional, that its software and applications were correctly installed and up-to-date, and that it was located in an environment which was correctly heated and ventilated, would ensure that it would work to optimal capacity. Fixing one of these things and ignoring the other two is not enough. The computer will not work correctly unless all three areas are fixed. And so it is with us as human beings.

These three things affect us all on a daily basis. Whether or not we are aware of it, the physical brain and our mental processes are working away in the background, influencing our actions and our decisions, and our social environment is all around us, also influencing the way that we think and the choices that we make. Therefore, it makes sense to look at all of these areas, both in light of what we have experienced in the past, and how they are working now.

As children, we learn by example, looking to the world around us for evidence to make sense of our experiences, and building up that store of information that we mentioned in the last chapter as a kind of reference library against which we judge everything that happens to us in the present. The context in which we are learning is both internal (our biology and mental processes) and external (for example the things people say to us, our own experiences, things we see in the media). To appreciate how you learned as you grew up, you need to understand that you did not develop in isolation as a person, but as part of that context. The physical components of your brain developed in a context. Your mental processes and reactions developed in a context. Your social skills and experience of interactions with other people, and the responses that you expect to get from them, all developed in a context. The context of your experience therefore affects both the workings of the brain itself, the way you perceive and react to situations and experiences, and the way in which you expect people to behave and to react to you.

Looking at the effect of this in your current life, you can understand that what you have experienced in the past will affect your reactions now. Physical changes happen in the brain as a response to habitual reactions. Beliefs and reactions (at a conscious level) and emotions and feelings (at a subconscious level) become automatic. Expectations of how we anticipate others will behave also become automatic, as we learn them by experience. At some point, if we are not getting the results that we want in life, we need to go back and look at our programming, in all three of these areas. We will do that later in this book. You should also understand that you are still learning, still developing, and still cataloguing, so if something is not working for you, you need first to understand where that reaction or belief came from, and then change it.

You should also take into account that no two people

are the same because no two contexts are the same. Even identical twins who have a 100% DNA match and grew up in the same household will have experienced different environments, and will have differences in personality. Therefore, it's not sensible to compare yourself to someone else and be critical that you have not achieved what they have achieved, because you are not the same person, and your contexts will not be the same. They will have advantages over you in some areas, and you over them in others.

In this book, we will look at all three of these areas, and how we can change them. For now, it's enough to understand that they have shaped the person that you are today, and will continue to shape the person that you are tomorrow. Therefore, it is critical to be able to work back in your life experience and see how they have contributed to your beliefs about yourself and to your self-concept. It's also critical to have some understanding of how they work, and how they can be shaped to better support the person that you want to become and the things that you want to achieve. Like the self-concept that you have, none of these things is fixed. They are all open to change. Currently, you may just be accepting whatever life throws at you, and allowing it to control all of these areas. You need to take control, or you will be like a car without a steering wheel. You'll go whichever way the road is sloping.

With this in mind, we'll take a closer look at your beliefs about yourself, and where these came from. Beliefs, as we have said, are biopsychosocially based. In spite of the fact that beliefs can be either conscious or subconscious, they are actually easier to understand than emotions. Therefore, this is a good starting point for you to begin to understand how you became the person that you are right now. In the next chapter, we will start to look at the underlying beliefs that make up your identity.

3 EXPLORING IDENTITY

Think back over what we've discussed so far. We've said that identity is a theory of ourselves, built from many sources. We've seen that these sources are both internal and external, from our physical brain, our thought processes, and our social environment. We have considered how we develop, first as children, but all through our lives, in the context of those three factors. Finally, we have considered how everything we experience is seen through that context, and how the conclusions that we make about the things we experience are stored away for future reference.

Keeping the above in mind, let's go back and look at all the beliefs that you wrote down about yourself in Chapter 1, and then expand upon them. You will want to take these beliefs into consideration when you answer the following questions. What we are going to do now is take a closer look at the things you believe about yourself which may be influencing your life, your relationships and your ability to achieve success (and by this, I mean whatever success means to you, not what you think the world believes it to mean). You are not restricted to answering these questions – if they lead you on to anything else which you feel is a fundamental question, please write it down, and think about your responses.

Here are some questions to start you off. I suggest you get a piece of paper to write your responses down on, as I don't want to set a limit of a number of lines for you to answer in. Your responses can be short, or pages – they should be as long as you need them to be to really consider the question and your response to it. Work through each section one at a time, writing down the heading, and then working through the section as laid out in the paragraphs below.

What are your talents?

The only unacceptable answer here is that you don't have any! Other than that, capture anything that you feel you are good at.

Look again at the third section, 'Skills', in Chapter 1. Your answers may range from career skills such as being good with numbers, organization or technical problems to being a great parent or carer, or really good at communicating with people. Every area where you feel confident or which comes to you naturally is a talent. If writing these down doesn't come easily, think about the moments in your life when you have been doing something and felt a real pleasure in your ability to do it.

Now think about why you believe you are good at these things. Is it because you've felt yourself that this is something that you're good at, or did someone tell you that this is a skill you have? If it's something you've been told, who or what told you? Was it exam scores, achieving in business, or something that people have said? Was being told enough for you, or did you need to feel it yourself? If it's because you were told, how many times did you need to be told – is once enough, or do you need ongoing evidence and external approval? What do you need to experience, in order to believe that you are talented at something?

What are you like as a person?

Look back at your answers to the second section, 'Characteristics' in Chapter 1. Then write down how you see yourself as a human being.

Once you have done this, consider where your thoughts about yourself come from. Are they things that you remember having felt or expressed, are they a general perception you have of yourself, or are they comments that other people have made about you? Do you really believe all of these things about yourself?

Once you are happy that your answers reflect your real view of yourself, look to see if you have you written down any answers that appear to contradict each other – for instance, you might have written down both 'laid-back' and 'stressed'. If so, think about the situations in which these characteristics come to the fore. Perhaps you are stressed in certain situations, such as your work environment, and laid back in others, such as at home with your family. Do you feel all of these things all the time? If you have written down 'caring', for example, are you caring with everyone, or only with certain people – perhaps with your own family, or with children, or those who are ill?

What do your friends think about you?

Look back at your answers in the previous section. If your friends saw your responses, do you think they would recognize the person described as you? How about your family, or work colleagues?

Remember how you considered whether or not you felt that you had all of these characteristics all of the time. Do some characteristics appear only in certain situations? What sort of situations make you feel like this?

Do you need to be relaxed and comfortable with the people around you to truly feel that you can be 'yourself'? Are these things genuinely you, or do you have to work at them? Do you feel certain situations force you to react in a certain way – perhaps you are forced into situations with some people where you feel you have to be in charge, but this does not come naturally to you? Do your friends see you as you see yourself, or do they see you as you want to appear?

What do you like about yourself / dislike about yourself?

This can be absolutely anything! Your thoughts in the sections above may be helpful to you as a starting point, but you can be more specific here.

For example, you might write "I love that I can make people happy, I smile a lot and this makes people around me smile too", or " I dislike that I keep meaning to start my own business, but I can't seem to make myself actually make the leap and do it". Or you can work through the things you wrote above, perhaps "I dislike that when I get in from work I am always tired and stressed, and that makes me short-tempered with my family" or "I like that I am always laid-back, no matter what the situation is I never let it get to me".

Think about all of the things that you have ever thought about yourself with either approval or annoyance. Why do the things that you like please you? How do they contribute to your enjoyment of life? Why do the things that you dislike annoy you? Are they stopping you doing something that you want to do, making you do things that you don't want to do, or holding you back in some way?

What makes you feel happy or sad?

Again, this can be anything at all – it can also be people. Once you have written down everything and everyone that has this effect on you, think about why that thing makes you feel this way.

Do the things that make you feel happy do so because they make you feel good, or make other people feel good, or because you are helping a cause or making a contribution? Do they make you feel good just because they reinforce that you have the ability to do them?

Do the things that make you feel bad do so because you don't really want to do them, because you have to do them, because you do then without meaning to, because you're not able to do something that you want to be able to do?

What are your interests?

Think of all your interests – areas that you like to study, hobbies that you like to take part in, a career or business that you would like to be involved in (and maybe you are involved in it already). What do you like about these things? How well do they line up to the responses you made in the 'Talents' section? Do any of them figure in the things that make you happy or sad? Do you like any of these things because you are good at them? If you're not good at them, and that makes you unhappy, is there something that you could do which would improve your ability?

Do your friends and family share these interests, and if so, is your own interest in them genuine, or do you take part in them because you want to share something with the people that you love? If the latter, do you genuinely have an interest and a satisfaction in it now, has this grown from participation?

How do you identify yourself?

This is something slightly different. You may identify yourself as one of a number of different groups, and some of these may mean more to you than others. The most obvious are probably gender, ethnic background, and sexual orientation.

Many people also respond with answers around class – "I am working class" and place of origin – "I am a Geordie." Some people may have a physical or mental handicap and identify themselves as 'disabled'. You may also identify yourself in terms of your outside interests and the social groups that this makes you a part of – "I am a biker/an academic/a member of the Labour Party".

Write down all of the groups to which you feel you belong. You will obviously be a member of some of these purely on the basis of your genetics – others you will have joined from preference or conviction.

Think about all of the groups with which you have identified yourself. Which of them please you, and which do not? How do you feel that these things affect yourself, and affect how others see you? Do you feel that any of these things hold you back, because of other people's perceptions of you, or because they give you a disadvantage?

Do you feel that you have the power to change any of these things if you are unhappy with them? Do you feel resentful of people's attitudes towards you in any of these areas?

Is there anything else that you feel fundamentally affects you?

This is your chance to put down anything else that you feel has an effect on your identity. It can be absolutely anything which has come to mind when you were working through the sections above. If you feel that it has an effect on how you see yourself and how others see you, it should be here.

What helps you? What holds you back?

For this section, I am not going to prompt you at all, because now we are getting down to the real crux of identity. You have written down answers to many of the things that affect people when they are considering their identity – both in terms of how they see themselves, and how others see them.

Working through those sections should have given rise

to a lot of thoughts about the things in your life that either help or hinder you. Without too much pause for thinking about it, write down two columns – things that are helping you to achieve your goals, and things that are holding you back.

What would you like to CHANGE?

You can't change the world in a day, but you can make a pretty fundamental change in your own life just by picking up one small thing that is stopping you moving forward, and deciding that you are not going to allow it to hold you back any more. It's much easier to work on one thing at a time, you will see much more benefit and get much more of a sense of achievement from putting your attention onto one thing than trying to change a multitude of things with a small amount of attention on each.

With that in mind, circle the one item from your 'hold me back' list that you feel causes the most problems in your life (if you think there are two things equally problematic for you, and if you feel they can be worked on together, then you can choose two – but no more!) Even if you are one of those people who likes to set the bar really high!

Now that we have looked at you, the person you are, and the many aspects that make up your identity, there is one more thing to consider before we move on to looking at understanding and challenging your beliefs. In the next section, we are going to look at your goals.

4 SETTING GOALS

Most people have goals. These can vary from random statements about something that you would 'like' to do in your life, to detailed plans of your objectives, complete with timescales, method statements, and means of measuring whether or not success has been achieved against the goal set. Even where the person has been very meticulous in setting out their goals, I have found that they are not always sure why each particular goal is important to them, or what it really means to them.

Goals are not always something that we want to achieve of and for themselves. When we start to look more deeply at why we want the things that we do, we often find that it's not the thing itself that we want, but what it means to us. For example, someone might state that they want a promotion at work, but not think about what this actually means to them. It might be that they want more money to buy a car they have set their mind on, to have more respect from their colleagues, or because they find their current position boring and need more of a challenge. When looked at in this way, it could be argued that the increased income, the greater respect, or the challenge, are actually the goals, rather than the promotion itself. The promotion is just the means to an end. Taking this one step further, you could ask if there was another and better way to achieve the goals.

Most of us are programmed, from an early age, by the examples we see around us and the things that we are told are the 'facts of life'. Many of us who listened to our parents grew up to think that there were certain 'correct' goals that it was necessary to follow to be 'successful'. These are usually around doing well at school, going to University, qualifying in subjects that would guarantee a good job, buying a house, getting married and having a family, and saving enough in your pension fund to guarantee a good retirement. Unfortunately, this does not work so well in the current financial climate, where school-leavers and graduates are struggling to find work, and people are being laid off when companies downsize or go under. The risk can be minimized by being a 'specialist' in a niche area, and certainly people who specialize to a great depth in a certain subject are often very well paid – however, the down side of this is there will be, by definition, less jobs in these areas, and in tough economic times these may be heavily fought over. Specializing too much can leave you unable to find work in your own subject area. Specializing too little can leave you fighting over one job with five hundred other people, all capable of doing exactly what you do.

The challenge to this way of thinking came with the Internet age. This was the time of the mass rise of the entrepreneur. Certainly, many people made their fortunes in this time of great change. A great proportion of these people made them and lost them. If you think about the dotcom boom, you will understand that it's possible to reach your goals, only to see everything slip through your fingers. The problem in many cases is that people don't have sufficient knowledge to back up their goals, or to secure them once they have attained them.

There is a lot of material that teaches how to focus on

your goals, visualize them, make positive affirmations about them, and to assume that you will be successful. Unfortunately, there is less literature pertaining to the number of times that people have failed. If you read biographies of hugely successful people, you will understand that many of them have suffered embarrassment, failure and bankruptcy, perhaps many times, before becoming successful. Some have made fortunes, lost them, and made them back. The difference with these people and those who feel that one failure means that they are not destined to be successful, is that they understand that a failure in one goal does not mean that you are a failure as a person. They are able to make the distinction between failing and being a failure. It also means that they were willing to study their subject, make decisions, act on them, and deal with any problems that arose, if and when they came along.

Another problem that I see constantly is caused by people reading the stories of others who imply that becoming "successful" is easy. This can lead you to question why you find it difficult to know where to start when others appear to have breezed into fame and fortune. It's true that some people do seem to have a knack for being in the right place at the right time, but if you start out thinking that a goal is easy, you're setting yourself up for being discouraged as soon as you hit your first challenge.

Whatever goal you set yourself, whether it's financial or not, you need to be realistic about the problems that you will face and will have to overcome – both problems coming from the outside, and problems coming from the inside, from your own thought patterns and biology. You also need to make sure that the goal you desire is worth any pain you experience on the way. Finally, you need to learn to see the path to your goal as enjoyable, rather than a struggle. If you anticipate that it will be painful and difficult, then that's very likely to be what you will experience.

The dictionary definition of a goal is 'the object of a person's ambition or effort; an aim or desired result'. Note that this does not say 'the aim of a person's wish, daydream or casual desire'. Effort is required, as is true ambition – saying 'I would like to win the lottery' or even 'I am going to win the lottery' isn't doing very much to further your goals, however well you affirm it. An aim is directed and focused, as in aiming an arrow. A desired result is something into which you are putting energy and emotion, maybe thinking it would be nice to have it, but failing to take any action to get it.

Once you understand this, you will understand why it is so critical to really understand the meaning behind your goals. If you are going to have to acquire knowledge, and put energy and effort into it, you will need motivation to keep you going. If you don't have a clear emotional desire around the thing that you want, where are you going to find your motivation when things become difficult and you are faced with a challenge? It's easier to say it wasn't meant to work out and just go and watch TV!

There is also a fundamental roadblock to fulfilling your greatest dreams, in that many people are living in a state of day-to-day survival, trying to meet all the demands of everyday life and not managing to make time to think about the things that would make them feel happy and fulfilled.

I am not suggesting that you throw caution to the winds, give up your business or your job, and go out in pursuit of your dreams – in fact, I find it worrying that some people advocate doing this. If you have no responsibilities, no dependents, and no real attachment to anything in your life that you might lose by doing so, that's fine. If you do your homework, weigh up your decisions and feel you're taking a calculated risk that's also fine. If you're really uncomfortable about doing it, then in most cases I would advise finding an alternative route to your goal.

There are exceptions, but most people find that living in a constant state of fear and anxiety is very bad for both their physical and mental health. Moving a little outside of our comfort zone is good for us and helps us to grow – throwing yourself head first into an area where you are completely out of your depth is not something that many people can handle. However, this does not mean that you cannot think about, plan and move towards your goals. You just need to make sure you do this in an environment where you keep some control of your outcomes and do not lose things that you are not prepared to give up to achieve them.

I would also like to stress that just because you are not willing to give up everything to go for your dreams, this does not mean that you are not deserving of getting them. Nor should you compare yourself unfavorably with people that do. We are all different – we have different comfort levels, different goals, different ways of thinking. Every goal requires some sort of sacrifice, even if it's only 10 minutes of your time every day – you are still giving something up to obtain something else. You need to work out what you are, and are not, willing to sacrifice to reach your goal.

Humans have certain needs in their lives. The fundamental need of a person is biological – such as the requirement for adequate nourishment, sleep and shelter. Beyond these are the need for security, the need to be loved and accepted, and the need to be respected both by others and by yourself. Sadly, even in the twenty-first century, many people, including some here in the UK, do not have even the fundamental biological requirements. It is difficult to focus on your goals when you are lacking in these basic aspects of human need.

Even if these requirements are met, it is still important to feel a sense of security, belonging, and being appreciated. Before starting to look at your higher level goals, think about your own feelings in all of the areas just listed. Are you comfortable in all of these things? If not, you should look at them first. What do you feel you need to be confident of being secure, accepted and respected? What evidence would you need to believe that this was the case? If you are not secure in any of these areas, what could you do to change that?

Assuming that you are happy that everything is fine for you in these areas, you can start to look at your goals. One question first though – are you sure that your goals are actually YOUR goals?

This may seem a strange question, but if you think back to the chapter on identity, you will see that this actually may not be the case. Remember how we said that identity is a theory of ourselves, which is built from many sources, and that some of these sources are external. I keep repeating this, and there's a good reason for that – this is something I have found people do not realize, and you absolutely have to know this if you are going to have a clear picture of what your motivations are.

Goals are a positive thing, but when you think about it, they imply that everything is not 100% perfect in your life – you want to have, do or be something that you currently don't have, don't do or are not. This is not a bad thing because, as others have said, as soon as you stop growing you begin to die – but it's still something that you have identified which is missing in your life, and which you truly feel you must have. The question that you need to ask yourself is – must you have it because you truly want it, understand your motivation to get it, and are willing to make the necessary sacrifices that you must make to get it? Or, do you want it because you are responding to someone else's expectation or benchmark that this is something that you must have to be successful, or attractive, or a winner, or whatever it is that you want to be?

Imagine that you were given, as a child, a description of what a 'man' should be like. If you were told that a man should be big, strong and capable, you may have issues if you're short, quiet and studious. If your parents had aspirations that you would own a multi-million pound corporation, and you own a successful small business, you might have a sneaking feeling that you're not really doing as well as you might, even if those around you tell you constantly how impressed they are by your success. If your parents spent lots of money on tennis coaching, and told all their friends that you were going to grow up to win Wimbledon, you could probably win a few county tournaments but still think you're not a good player, unless you can win a grand slam.

What you need to be aware of here is that it's not what other people think that matters – it's what you think yourself. Other people may pass judgment on you, or praise or blame you, but if you don't take on what they are saying, that doesn't matter. It's the things that we accept as being the truth, and store away in the reference library in our heads, that matter. We may not even be consciously aware of them, but we will draw on them for information when making decisions, and these decisions include the goals that we set for ourselves.

One of the founders of humanistic psychology, Carl Rogers, highlighted the issue of *incongruence*. This is where try to shape ourselves to the expectations of others, trying to become the person that we feel others expect us to be, rather than following our own desires. Rogers believed that the foundation of these problems was the fact that we will learn to believe that the love and affection of others for us is contingent on us meeting these conditions.

In the examples above, you may subconsciously feel that the love of your parents or the affection of your friends depends on you being 'manly', exceedingly rich, or a famous tennis player. This may not be rational when you think about it in these terms, but the subconscious is not always rational! If you subconsciously believe these things, they will mould your goals without you even being aware of it. The sad thing is that striving for goals to try to achieve a sense of self-worth rarely works, because the goals are never enough. The issue is with the sense of identity, not with personal achievement.

Rogers used a technique called "person-centered counseling", in which the therapist would show unconditional regard for the client – that is, would be warm and respectful towards them, no matter what opinions they expressed. This was shown to reduce the number of times that a person would speak negatively about themselves. In the same spirit, make sure that you are looking at your goals as things that you wish to achieve that will make you happy – they should not be either a stick with which to beat yourself, or a measure of how well you come up to someone else's expectations.

I would like to add here that this process should not be about blame. Not only is blame a very unhelpful emotion, in many cases the person you may feel is responsible for any incongruence you have may have been genuinely proud of you and trying to push you to make the best life possible for yourself – or you may be acting on a completely random remark that has stayed with you through life, even though you don't remember it.

There are two key things to keep in mind here. One is that it's much more helpful to look forward than to look back. When looking at your goals, work both for congruence with yourself, and for improvements that you, personally, desire. Focus on growth and development of yourself as a person rather than dwelling on past events (although we will look at these later in the book, and how they may have shaped the person you are today, they should be looked at as a means of understanding, not as a basis for blame or a denial of responsibility for your own actions).

What we are seeking to do here is to gain enough understanding and confidence to be able to set goals, understand motivations, and explore opportunities.

IT'S ALL IN YOUR MIND

Before you go on to look at your own personal goals, let's summarize what has been discussed in this chapter.

We've said that the goal itself is usually not the main aim but the means to an end, and that it's important to understand the true motivation behind having that goal. We must evaluate the reason that we really want it, and consider whether there is another, better way of achieving the true desire.

We've talked about how we can be influenced by our parents, friends and the example of other people to set goals based on what they do or say to us, and how this influences our beliefs about what our goals should be.

We've discussed the effort that is needed to attain goals, and therefore why we need to be so clear about what we are trying to achieve, and why.

We've mentioned the problems caused by needing to make sure that we have our everyday basic needs met before we can fully concentrate on goals (if something is missing here, it could be a goal to achieve it).

Finally, we have discussed how the goals that we have can actually be formed by impressions from other people of what we *should* aspire to, and how this can lead to incongruence.

With all of the above in mind, you should now start to write down your goals. I would advise you to set only one restriction on yourself here, and that it to understand that there are some physical limitations on goals. To use an extreme example, if you're 112 years old, it would be a waste of energy which could be better spent if you are aspiring to win the next Miss World contest.

Other than that, write down all of your goals – absolutely everything that you really, really want to have, do, or be.

MY GOALS

_____

With the background information above in your mind, think about each of the goals that you have written down.

What does this goal mean to you? If your goal is to have a million pounds, what do you associate with that? What do you think of when you think of being a millionaire? Pleasure? Security? Freedom? Perhaps when you think about it, you may say that you want it, but have associations in your head around arguments with your spouse, losing your friends, or not being able to manage that amount of money – in other words, fear emotions. If this is really a goal, the desire must outweigh the fear, either because you make the desire stronger, or you control the fear. We will discuss changing our emotional reaction to things in Chapter 11 – but for now, you must be aware of this.

Why do you want this? Is it for yourself, or to meet expectations, or to prove something to the world, or because it's something you know would make someone else happy? Remember, what you want is not the thing itself, it's the association, the feeling it gives you. Do you want to lose weight? Get fit? Have a lovely house, car or boat? Take a degree? Start a business? WHY? What would that make you feel?

What would you have to give up to achieve this goal? Is the trade-off worth it?

What are you good at, and what do you enjoy? Are any of your goals around things you don't enjoy but feel you should? You might want to ask yourself why this is. You can achieve success in things that you don't naturally excel at, but it's much more enjoyable to do something you like and are good at.

Look back at the beliefs about yourself in Chapter 3. Look at the things that you consider to hold you back. Which of them hold you back in terms of achieving your goals? You may have written at least one of these down as things that you would like to change about yourself. If you haven't, you may want to reconsider what you feel is holding you back.

This is the end of the first section. Now that you've had chance to consider yourself and your goals as they are at the moment, we will move on to look in more depth at the reason behind these ways of thinking, which will allow you to take more control of your life and make the choices that you wish to make.

5 REALITY

There is first and foremost one thing that you need to understand about reality – it's not real! Or at least, it's only real in terms of it being your own experience and interpretation of the world.

What I mean by this is that reality is subjective. If you put two people into an identical situation, they will see and understand it differently, their experience of the situation will not be the same. Depending on their own personality, beliefs and knowledge, they will see different challenges or opportunities and feel different levels of comfort or discomfort. In fact, they will not even see the situation in an identical way. Therefore, reality is subjective because it's colored by the person experiencing it.

Your views about yourself are just that: views. Yes, they are based on experience, from the things that you have felt and the things that people have said about you, but that does not make them a concrete fact. They will have been put together through your unique biopsychosocial perspective. One person having a fear of water may feel embarrassment about this, and interpret it as weakness or cowardice. Another person with the same dislike of water may interpret this as a very sensible fear of

IT'S ALL IN YOUR MIND

drowning.

Someone else who has been through identical experiences to you will interpret them in their own unique way. They will not write down exactly the same things that you wrote when you listed your attributes, characteristics and skills, however similar their life has been to yours.

In the same way that we said that identity is a theory of yourself which is based on information from multiple sources, your other beliefs about people and things are also based on information from multiple sources. These sources are built up through the things that you see, hear and experience, and as you might guess, like your theories about yourself they are stored in that filing cabinet inside your head for future use. When something happens to you, you will assess the situation using both the incoming information that you are receiving at the time (such as what you are seeing or hearing) and the information you already hold in your internal reference library. This doesn't mean that your interpretation of people and situations is "real". It just means that something or someone in the past caused you to store information in your mind which makes you interpret them in that way.

Think of two people approaching a dog in the street. One of these people was previously bitten by another dog, and this experience has registered inside his head. He will probably feel nervous of getting too near to the dog; he may feel a sense of anxiety, experience physical symptoms like sweating, and may take evasive action such as crossing the street to avoid the dog.

The other person has had nothing but happy experiences with dogs; unless the dog is behaving in a way that may make him feel threatened, he will probably walk past it quite happily and without experiencing any of the negative thoughts and physical symptoms that the first man has. He may stop to pat the dog, if it looks friendly. Then again, he may not even notice that there is a dog. He has no reason to be paying particular attention to a dog in his path.

Now imagine that there is a third person approaching the dog. He has no very strong feelings about dogs one way or another; he has never been bitten, and he has never had a dog of his own. Would you expect him to avoid the dog, walk past the dog, or to notice the dog at all?

There are several things that may affect the third man's reaction. If the dog is acting aggressively, perhaps barking or growling, he may assess that it's a threat from what he sees and hears, and move out of its way. If there is something unusual about the dog, for example that it is very large, he may notice it because it's something out of the ordinary. If it is a very average dog, and not behaving in such a way as to draw attention to itself, what he does will depend largely on what information he has inside his head. If he has watched something on TV involving a person being attacked by a dog, or if someone in the past has told him a vivid story about being bitten, he may feel nervous and move out of the way – even if he isn't aware of why he is doing it.

When you think about this, you will see that he is reacting to something he has never experienced himself, but even so he has information in his head that has caused a reaction. Our reactions can be based purely on hearsay, on things that we have never actually experienced ourselves, especially if the information has come from what we consider to be a trusted source – such as a parent or teacher in childhood, or a respected colleague or 'expert' in the related field when we are an adult.

If you think about it, it's logical to learn this way. When you were a baby, you knew none of these things; you had no fear of failure, or being rejected, or of embarrassing yourself. Absolutely everything that you have learned, you have learned from either personal experience or external sources. The big question you might then ask yourself is, how do I know that the information I have is correct?

The problem with this is that in a lot of cases there is no such thing as 'correct'. Like reality, to a certain degree it must be subjective. There are levels and degrees of correctness in most of the more complicated pieces of information that we hold. Some things are obviously correct, but this is usually fairly simple data such as 'grass is green' or 'fire is hot'. Even a relatively simple scenario like the dog example above can be more complicated than it initially appears.

Think about the information that we have considered. There is no 'correct' answer to the question 'Do dogs bite?' Some dogs may bite, some may not. Some dogs may bite in a certain situation, such as if a burglar breaks into their house. Some dogs may never have bitten, may not be expected even by their owners to bite, but will suddenly bite someone for no apparent reason. You cannot give a 'yes' or 'no' answer to the question "Will that dog bite me?" based solely on the fact that it's a dog. And yet, it's possibly to have an immediate, unconscious response to the dog based on an expectation that it will bite, purely because it's a dog.

The reality of whether dogs bite depends on the situation and the dog. The best answer you can give is 'sometimes', and make sure you have all of the relevant information about what makes dogs bite and how they might act if they were going to do so. If you act in a way that makes a dog feel threatened, it's more likely to bite you, and you may consider it 'reality' that dogs bite. If you change the way that you act, you are then effectively changing your reality.

Of course, some things may be 'correct' as we know them at the time, but then may turn out not to be correct at all. At one time, it was an accepted fact that the Earth is flat. It was also accepted that the sun moves round the Earth. These were 'facts' to scientists of the time, they were not disputed for many years. Now, of course, we are aware that these supposed 'facts' were actually incorrect.

You may have lots of 'facts' in your head about yourself and other people which are not sound, or which are no longer true. Whether or not you realize that they are there, you will be using them to assess things that happen to you now, and they will affect your decisions.

Hopefully, it will be of help to you to understand that these things are not actually real, that they are only your stored perceptions and interpretations of past events and experiences. We learn by repetition, and by compiling information from what we believe are the best sources at the time, storing conclusions and carrying out judgments. This does not mean that they are necessarily the best sources, or that you are storing helpful conclusions! You have the ability to challenge the things that you have stored, and to replace them with things that are better able to support your goals and challenges. You need to have confidence in your ability to do this.

So, where might the problems with your stored information lie?

For a start, you may not be listening to the right people. Let's use someone going into business as an example. There are some very intelligent people in the world who nevertheless do not have a clue about the area you want to learn about. If you listen to them while they are speaking about their own field, great. However, just because they excel in one area, beware of thinking that they know everything about everything! However intelligent they are, however brilliant in their own area, however much of a role model you consider them to be, if they have not actually done something themselves, they are not an 'expert' in it. They may have their own ideas or theories about your area or field, but unless these have been gained through personal experience, they are just as likely to be based on false conclusions as your own ideas and theories.

Think about it – if an obese salesperson approached you offering a franchise to sell a miracle weight loss pill, would you join up with them? The answer to that one is fairly obvious – most people would assume either that the pill did not work, or that there was some reason for the salesperson not to take it themselves, and would not buy.

Here's a question where the answer is a little less obvious – if someone who had built a successful business selling cars offered to mentor you in building a local business grooming dogs, would you pay for the mentorship?

That one is slightly more complex, and it depends to a large extent on how you see that person. If you see her a successful businesswoman, you might take the mentorship. If you see her as an expert in car sales, but also as someone who knows nothing about dog grooming, you might not. Maybe you'll think that the area you need mentoring in is sales and marketing, and will be indifferent as to whether you are in the same industry because you admire her skill in this area – or alternatively, you may think that this being the case, you would be better taking a mentorship with a sales and marketing expert.

If you think about this scenario, there are four different beliefs about the same person. The person is not changed, but the assessment of her ability to help you lies in your belief system.

If you are one of those people who is very impressed by others and thinks that you're pretty average; if you take at face value most of the things that people say to you, without ever challenging or asking for evidence, you may be setting yourself up for a fall. Many people have been talked into handing over money to a clever conman with a good sales talk, and have lost their investment. On the other hand, if you are someone who is skeptical of everything or everyone, you may miss out on a number of opportunities, purely because you refuse to listen to them and assess them. In the same way, if you are very confident in yourself and your own abilities, you are much more likely to take risks than someone who is not.

Think now about the beliefs that you have about

people in general, and yourself in particular. The point here is not that either of these ways of thinking is right or wrong, but that it will affect how you deal with people, and you should be aware of it. Are your thoughts here holding you back? Where did these thoughts come from? Is there something which you consider to be reality which is actually made up purely of your own beliefs and stored experiences, but which is holding you back – either because of what it makes you believe about yourself, or about other people and situations?

As you know, you learned your beliefs from the people around you: your parents, friends, siblings, teachers, schoolfellows, what you heard on the news, what you saw on the TV, what you read in books, the things that you have experienced ... with such a vast amount of sources, is it any wonder that we don't always know where they came from? You will overwrite this information over time as you receive what you feel to be "better" information. Some beliefs about what is reality, however, are really deep-rooted, and these are hard to overwrite.

Think now of any really strongly held beliefs that you have. Do you know where these may have come from? Do you remember your parents discussing the subject with you when you were young? Do you remember an experience that had a really strong effect on you?

Once you really start to think about your beliefs, and understand that this is what they are, then you can start to change the ones that cause you issues. As I said earlier, once you can do that, you are effectively changing your own reality.

If, for example, you believe that you are not academically gifted, why do you think that? Did you fail an important exam? Did a teacher tell you that you would never achieve? Did you grow up in the shadow of a brilliant sibling? If you think about it, none of these things actually *proves* that you don't have academic ability, but any one of them may be enough for you to think of yourself in that way.

The good thing about the mind is that it will take a new reference if you can provide one. What if you decided to give yourself a chance? Surrounded yourself with people who encouraged you to go out and start studying? Decided to prove your teacher wrong? If you can give yourself new evidence of your own abilities, your mind will be happy to replace the old information. The hardest part is often having the confidence in yourself to make the decision and take the first step.

You can apply this to any belief that you have: that you can't lose weight, make friends, find a lifelong partner, start a business, get a promotion. Very little in life is set in stone, but if you are not willing to challenge your negative beliefs, some things may as well be. Look back at your goals. Which of those do you not believe you can do because you have a negative belief about yourself and your abilities? Can you understand that your beliefs are not reality?

One of the most dangerous things about this information in your head is that it can lead to many missed opportunities. The human mind is not capable of processing everything that we take in through our senses, and therefore we have to filter out some of the information around us. The process by which we do this is known as Attention. Most of us have been told at some stage, usually by parents or teachers, to "Pay attention!" but we still may be unaware of why this is important. Paying attention does not just mean to listen to whatever lecture or telling off you may be getting – you can do that and still not take it in, as I am sure you are aware! Attention is a selection process which operates between what your senses pick up and what actually reaches your brain for processing.

This is the reason that we all perceive things differently, above and beyond the relative ability of our eyes and ears.

The question you will probably be asking now is, what creates those filters that are carried out through the process of attention? Again, this would be influenced by your biopsychosocial experience. We all have genes, and therefore there is a biological and genetic influence on our experience. We are also influenced by our cognitive processes, which as discussed we have learned throughout our lives, and very heavily by the social environment, which will have affected how we see both ourselves and others, and our expectations. Therefore, you can say that perception is influenced by knowledge and shared experience, as well as by biology.

Now combine this with the idea that we cannot process all of the information we sense, that a lot of information will inevitably be lost between your sensation and your conscious awareness, due to the existence of these attentional filters. How does this affect you?

For a start, if you are constantly focusing on the bad, and expecting that bad things will happen, where is your attention? It's on the bad. So, if something good happens, you might not even notice – and if you do, you might think it's a one-off, and not register it as evidence that not only bad things happen. The end result of that way of thinking is that you continue to believe that you are unlucky, that only bad things happen to you – and will continue to do so no matter how many times something good happens to you.

You will also be one of the glass-half-empty people who always see the bad in everything. When some opportunity arises, do you even see the opportunity, or do you just see all the things that could go wrong if you go for it?

As an example, imagine that you would like start investing in property. You talk about it a lot with your friends, you watch a few programs on TV, you look on a few websites and you read a newspaper article or two. If you gave your email address on one of the websites, you maybe start getting mails offering you investment opportunities. What do you do with these?

You would be surprised how many people delete these emails without even reading them – including many people who want to invest in property! Why? For a number of reasons, and many of them are based purely on beliefs.

For example, you may believe that every dealer in property is a crook, and that all of these emails will be a scam. There is some basis for believing this; there have been many public cases of people being conned out of money recently (and not just in property). However, it's highly unlikely that everyone selling property is a crook!

You may also have deleted the email because you don't think the property market is secure or that property is a good investment at the moment; this is also based on beliefs, but on more specific beliefs. Why do you think this? If it's because a neighbor you ran into when he was collecting his newspaper told you so, then he may not really be qualified to advise you! Of course, he may be a long term property investor who has told you that investing in property does not meet your current investment strategy, in which case you might consider that his opinion is worth listening to! You may also have decided this for yourself, based on a lot of research and knowledge building around this area of investment, and that's fine.

I'm not saying don't trust any other sources. You just need to make sure that you are happy that any source you're listening to is reliable, and that you have a good reason for having this belief.

Beyond belief in these external sources, you also have beliefs about yourself. If you would love to invest in property, but are deleting these emails because you don't believe you are capable of doing so, why? Everyone who invests in property is not a multi-talented super-genius. Like investors in most areas, property investors have a variety of talents and capabilities. They are people, like you, with strengths and weaknesses. Good investors learn from each other, from books, from reputable sources of information, and by experience, which can only be gained from going out and doing it. Why do you think that you can't do something that others are doing successfully?

If you read the email, you may of course decide that this is not the right investment for you, perhaps needing too much money to be put in upfront, or something that you feel to be risky. Again, you are working on a belief, but a pretty solid one. You've obviously got enough knowledge to be able to make that decision.

Here is a key factor – obtaining knowledge from the right sources. So, if you find the right people to speak to about your 'problem' area, do you think that might change your beliefs? If you have joined a property group and spent a lot of time speaking to experienced people, and if one day you realize that you are understanding all of the conversations, and your mind is supplying your own opinion on them (and maybe you're even helping out someone else!) might your belief about your ability have changed? You can be fairly sure that it would. You have changed your beliefs by taking specific action. Next time you see a property deal, you will probably assess it. You might not buy it, but you will have the knowledge to make an informed decision.

Does this principle work in other areas of your life? Absolutely! If you believe you're a 'fat person' who will 'always be fat', then you get a personal trainer, start eating healthily and begin to lose weight, will you have changed your belief? You certainly have evidence that you have some control over your weight.

If you think that you can't make friends because you've had bad experiences in the past, try changing your belief from 'nobody likes me' to 'it's unrealistic to assume that everyone will like me'. Then try to make yourself pleasant and cheerful. Make sure you listen to people instead of just talking to them. Smile at people when you meet them.

There's a pretty good chance that you will start to get better responses – and both your beliefs about your own likeability and about the friendliness of other people will improve.

If you want a promotion, start looking at the people doing the role that you want. What skills do they have, what knowledge do they need? Educate yourself as much as you can in the area. When you feel confident, speak to your manager and volunteer to take on some tasks which relate to the role you want. This gives you chance to prove your ability (both to your manager and also to yourself!) and gets you some free experience in this area. After you have proved that you can do the work, how much likelier are you to get the role – either at your existing company, or if you applied for that role with another employer?

I have done this a number of times and I can assure you that it works. It also changes your belief about your ability to do the job and therefore to get the promotion. You've given yourself evidence that this is the case.

To sum up then, we have a limited ability to process information, and much of what our senses take in will not get as far as our perception. What we process and what is discarded is determined by our filters, the end product being a combination of what we have actually sensed and the stored information that we hold. Filters are built up through a combination of our genetics, our learned beliefs and our social conditioning. Past experience is a filter, it will affect how you view the things that happen in your life, and may be why you think you can't do it, don't act on it or don't even notice it! Attention is also a filter, and we can control where we focus it. If your mind is always focusing on the negative and expecting bad things to happen, you won't be able to notice, or process, the good, it will be filtered out before it gets through. Also bear in mind that attention can be allocated consciously as well as unconsciously, which is why it is so important to modify the beliefs that are holding you back. It's hard to be cheerful and positive if your mind has trained itself to always expect the worst!

You need to be aware of the beliefs that are stored subconsciously in your mind, as they make up your own version of what you know as Reality. This is not something that many of us naturally question. Start to question it now. What beliefs do you have about the things you want? Are they valid, and are they useful? Do you need to change them? Attentional control is a skill that can be learned and modified, but to do so you need to have a solid belief system in place.

If you can do this, you really do have the power to change your own reality,

In chapter 8, we will take a close look at beliefs and how they shape our world. For now, it's enough to understand that our beliefs do not make a set-in-stone reality – neither the beliefs or the reality are permanently fixed. Before doing that, in the next two chapters, we will look at two of the key factors that control how we form our beliefs, and get a better understanding, through seeing what made them, as to how we can change them. The first of these, and one which will definitely have had an influence on you during your life to date, is conditioning.

6 CONDITIONING

We are conditioned every day by our experience, usually without being aware of it. It has been happening since the day you were born. Conditioning is an underlying foundation of your belief system, and it works in two different ways.

Classical conditioning builds associations in your mind about what may be connected to certain people, places and experiences. It creates expectations about what will happen. You have probably heard of 'Pavlov's dogs', the study which led to the discovery of classical conditioning. Ivan Pavlov, a Russian physiologist, was investigating salivation in dogs when he noticed an interesting phenomenon. The dogs would salivate when food was brought in, an automatic and unconscious physiological response – but also, the dogs began to salivate whenever Pavlov's assistants entered the room. This could not be an automatic physiological response – dogs don't usually salivate when humans appear! Pavlov began to investigate why this would happen, and came to the conclusion that the dogs were salivating when they saw the assistants' white lab coats, which they would also wear when feeding the dogs. The lab coats had become associated in the mind of the dogs with being fed, to the point where they would salivate merely at the appearance of the coats.

This raised an interesting question – how did the dogs make the connection between the coats and the food? Pavlov considered that this must be a learned response, and carried out investigations which involved ringing a bell just before feeding the dogs. Sure enough, after a short period of time, the dogs began to salivate whenever they heard the bell. The food, an unconditional stimulus, had been paired in their minds with the bell, which then became a conditional stimulus, which is simply something which caused the dogs to have a conditional response – that is, a response would not have occurred without the pairing, i.e. salivation would not normally occur when hearing the bell.

Some people may not like to hear this, but regardless of our sophisticated thought processes, classical conditioning works in exactly the same way for humans as for dogs. We subconsciously make pairings between things in our minds, and this leads to automatic, subconscious reactions to the conditional stimulus.

As a simple example, let's take snow. Personally, I am a hot weather person, I love the summer and I really don't like being cold. Also, when living in a mountainous part of Scotland, I got stuck in the snow a few times (and have even seen the snow plough get stuck when it's really bad), and the whole family has been snowed in on several occasions. When I hear impending snow announced, I get that sinking feeling.

A friend of mine, on the other hand, is ecstatic when he hears there's going to be snow. He's a keen snowboarder. The difference here is not the snow – which is just snow, after all – it's what we associate it with. I pair it with inconvenience and having to wear multiple layers of clothes. He associates it with a lot of fun. When snow is announced, that's what we think about – and that thought

IT'S ALL IN YOUR MIND

is what creates the physical reaction, not the snow itself.

Because I don't like automatic reactions that make me feel bad, I decided to work on this. I thought of all the good things that can be associated with snow. For a start, it's very pretty – the inconvenience caused by living five miles from the nearest shop in bad weather is mitigated by the fact that we bought that house for the thirty mile view to the mountains, and in the snow it's unbelievably beautiful. Then there are the benefits of curling up in front of an open fire. And of course, there is Christmas. So now, when I heard that snow was forecast, the automatic reaction of dreading the cold and the inconvenience – which are of course valid points – were immediately overlaid by anticipating looking out of the window at the incredible view, with a huge open fire roaring in the background – and a lovely quiet Christmas week with my family.

If you think about the effects that might occur from having unhelpful pairings in your mind, you can begin to understand just how much of a difference could be made by changing the pairings for something more helpful. For example, if you have a pairing between asking someone out for dinner and embarrassment, this isn't likely to give you confidence to approach someone that you would like to go out with you!

How might you have made the pairing? Like the dogs and the bell, it is learned through experience. If you have had bad experiences, or a number of people have related bad experiences to you, the pairing will happen at a subconscious level. When you think of asking someone out, or it is suggested to you that you should do so, you will experience a negative reaction – quite often an unpleasant physical reaction can happen, similar to stomach cramps before an exam. You need to understand that the reaction is not to the date, it's to the fear of embarrassment that you have linked to it.

The same feeling before an exam would be paired with

a fear of failing – think about it, if you're very confident of passing an exam, you don't get the same nervous effects as you would do if you thought you were not going to do well.

The strength of classical conditioning has been proved in trials which form the basis of aversion therapy treatments, which are to combat behaviors such as smoking, drinking and other unwanted habits. Animals who have eaten a food which has had unpleasant substances introduced, such as something which causes sickness and nausea, will stop taking that food, even when the substance has been removed. A pairing has been created between the food and illness, and they have developed an aversion to it. In the same way, if we have associated, for example, becoming self-employed with loss of security, difficult workload and possible bankruptcy, it will create a very different subconscious reaction to the one you would get if you had associated it with freedom, choice of hours worked and financial success.

The good news is that pairings can be broken and new ones formed. It is very important to be aware of this, because as I have said, classical conditioning works at a subconscious level. The reaction does not come at the end of a conscious thought process, it happens automatically. Therefore, to change your associations, you first need to be aware of them, and then you need to work at creating new pairings.

At a fundamental level, some people are naturally happy and optimistic, and some are naturally depressed and pessimistic. If you are a person who always starts the day feeling unenthusiastic, or automatically thinks about the worst thing that could happen when being told of an event or an opportunity, you need to stop this RIGHT NOW. You are doing yourself huge damage on both a physical and a mental level. You need to get into the habit of consciously intercepting your own subconscious reactions. Your brain is a very sophisticated computer, and you have control over your own programming. Begin to notice when you feel unhappy or fearful. What was going through your mind to cause that reaction? How might you think about it differently?

A really good habit which I always recommend to people is to sit down periodically and think about all the things in your life that you are grateful for. Even if it's only that the sun is out, or that you saw a wonderful sunset, or a lovely view, it's something that made you happy. Practice thinking about the things that make you happy rather than the things that make you sad. Get used to focusing on things that make you feel a sense of happiness and contentment. If you do this regularly, your subconscious reactions will automatically begin to become more positive.

To this point, we have only considered our subconscious reactions, and the classical conditioning that lies behind them. However, as humans, with complex mental processes and the ability to assess our reactions and the results of them, we also have to consider the conscious aspects of our programming.

Operant conditioning is a phenomenon discovered by behaviorist B.F. Skinner, who conducted experiments in which he observed the behavior of rats in a maze. Skinner's theory was simple – behavior is modified by the responses that you expect to get from it. Positive responses will reinforce the behavior, making it more likely to occur. Negative responses will decrease the likelihood of the behavior occurring.

Responses which increase the likelihood of the behavior occurring are known as reinforcers. They can be positive (in that they make something good happen) or negative (in that they stop something bad happening). Things that stop the behavior happening are logically known as punishers – they are something that you do not want to happen.

In Skinner's experiments, rats quickly learned to push a button to release a pellet of food. This is a conscious choice on the part of the rat – it has learned that this behavior will obtain a reward (the food) and so it carries out the behavior more often.

If you have children, you probably use this system without being aware of it. If you want your kids to do something, you might offer a reward, or warn of a punishment. For example, if you want them to do well in their exams, you might offer them some money for each exam passed. This would be a positive reinforcer, the intention being to increase the behavior that you want, in this case probably putting in a lot of revision time and paying attention at school. You might tell them that they had to attend evening coaching sessions if they failed certain exams, which is a negative reinforcer – putting in the revision time removes the awful thought of having to spend evening X-Box time studying maths! You might also threaten a punishment if they refused to put in the revision time, such as washing up for a month.

You might be interested to know that both Skinner and subsequent behaviorists have generally found that reinforcers work much more effectively than punishers in ensuring that a behavior is repeated. Evidence has also been found to support the theory that punishment can have side effects – your children might study if you threaten them with punishment, but other unwanted behaviors may take the place of being lazy with revision. The moral of the story seems to be to use reinforcement where possible. Given that traditionally punishment was used more often than reinforcement to produce desired behaviors in children, it can be interesting to think about what unhelpful behaviors you might have picked up in place of a behavior you stopped due to threat of punishment!

It is important to remember that conscious and unconscious responses cannot be thought of as completely separate entities. Your conscious thoughts control, to a certain degree, your subconscious programming. Your subconscious programming influences your conscious reactions. The things that you do and the responses that you make will all be affected by both your conscious and subconscious conditioning.

For example, many phobias are a combined result of classical and operant conditioning. Classical conditioning can create phobias, causing irrational fears of something completely harmless. Operant conditioning can reinforce that fear. For example, say that you are scared of mice. Classical conditioning will cause the reaction that creates a fear response. If you run away from the mouse, the fear reduces. If you think back to what we have discussed about operant conditioning, you'll see that you are giving a reinforcement – the fear goes away once the mouse is out of sight. This is negative reinforcement, and by doing it, you will learn that running away from the mouse is a good thing, because it makes the feeling of fear go away.

The fact that conscious and subconscious affect each other is a good thing. Consciously taking control of your thought processes allows you to influence your subconscious to respond more positively. Once you are getting more positive subconscious responses, these will create more positive conscious thoughts. However, this can also create complications. Our dog, Ozzy, is a really good example of this.

Some time ago, we bought Ozzy because he was in danger of ending up in a shelter, and we wanted to make sure he came to a home where his problems could be worked through. He was a young Dobermann, who unfortunately had issues with aggression, both to people and to other dogs. It quickly became apparent that his real issue was fear – the aggression was all fear related. He was very gentle towards the family, although quite timid and nervous at first. However, he responded very threateningly to any dog that was aggressive to him, and to callers at the door. He had obviously been badly treated by both animals and other dogs – he had a large scar on his leg which was clearly the result of a bite, was underweight, and flinched and cowered at any fast movements towards him.

To work with Ozzy, it was necessary to overcome the conditioning that had caused him to see strange humans and other dogs as a threat. On the surface, this might seem simple, but given that both classical and operant conditioning play a part in evoking responses, it becomes slightly more complicated.

Consider Ozzy's response to strangers, which was something that we needed to stop very quickly (most people get alarmed when 25 kg of Dobermann is straining at his lead, and barking and snarling – plus it's not much fun for the person hanging onto him either!) Being a dog, Ozzy operates on learned reactions, and given his behavioral responses, it was obvious that in his classical conditioning there was a pairing between people and pain. It was quite easy to tell that someone has obviously hit him at some stage, given that he would flinch any time someone raised a hand, even if they intended to stroke him.

Obviously, it was a good thing to change the association between people and pain, given that we wanted Ozzy to feel happy and relaxed around people. To remove an old pairing, you would make another pairing, say between people and treats. Therefore, you might say that when a strange person arrives, and he responds badly, you might give him a treat – therefore creating a new pairing which makes him associate people with treats. In theory, this should mean that Ozzy will become less likely to be aggressive towards people arriving at the door, because treats, unlike pain, are not threatening.

However, now think of operant conditioning. If Ozzy is snarling at an innocent passer-by, and I give him a treat, what am I doing? I am providing a positive reinforcement for the behavior, and if I reward him for it, I am making it more likely to happen. Not ideal.

There is a lot of material about on this subject, but as I was doing a biological psychology module at the time, I decided to do my own investigations. The conclusion I came to was that the critical point is to assess the behavior, and see if it is conscious or unconscious. What has worked with Ozzy is to deal with his subconscious reactions with classical conditioning, and his conscious reactions with operant conditioning. Barking at strangers seemed to be an involuntary response to the fear, so we would walk him off, speaking calmly, and praising him as he calmed down. Behaviors that we wanted him to learn were dealt with using operant conditioning, rewarding with treats and praise.

The thing that you need to learn is to identify whether each piece of conditioning that is affecting you getting to where you want to be is classical or operant. If, for example, you find that certain events, places or things trigger an involuntary emotional response, this is classical conditioning. If you feel that you have to carry out a certain behavior, or act in a certain way, this is operant conditioning.

Classical conditioning can make us react in strange ways if we don't understand the reasons for it. For example, I love the smell of WD40, it always makes me smile. That would seem really bizarre if I didn't remember that I associate it with my first ever bike rally, many years ago. It rained all weekend, and by the time that everyone was leaving, the whole field smelled of WD40! When you think about instinctive reactions that you have to people, places or things, can you remember why you might have them? Do you smile when you hear certain songs, or the theme tune to a TV program you liked when you were younger? If so, think about what you associate with that, and the feelings that you have when you hear it. This also works in a negative way; certain sounds, sights or smells can make us feel bad, without us always understanding why.

What about operant conditioning? It was always impressed upon me when I was younger that it was correct to speak quietly and politely to people. This was considered to be good behavior, and good behavior led to praise and pocket money! Even now, I hate to yell, and I don't like to be confrontational, even though I am pretty forceful about the things I need to be done. With time, I have learned to be persistent, but I still don't like confrontations. Operant conditioning can be the cause of a number of behaviors that you still carry out today. Looking at ways that you behave which you don't like, can you remember being rewarded for them when you were younger, or punished if you did not behave in that way?

The main thing you need to take from this chapter is the knowledge that you *learned* all of this conditioning – both classical and operant - and once you are aware of it you can relearn it in a more helpful way. Take some time to reflect on those things that have caused you to think and react as you do. Look to find more positive responses. Actively be aware of your reactions and the reasons for them, and condition yourself to notice when you are having a reaction you don't like. Learn to have a better reaction ready to replace it.

Remember, your current conditioning got you to the place where you are now. If you don't like it, you need to make some changes. Until you understand the source of your feelings and responses, and exercise some control over them, you are the mercy of your past.

Conditioning is not the only force that operates on us as we live and learn. Stereotyping also has a powerful effect on how we think and feel. We will look at this in the next chapter.

7 STEREOTYPING

Everyone has heard the word 'stereotyping'. We often use it to imply that someone has made a judgment about another person based on their appearance or their social group. When we say that someone is stereotyping, we usually mean this as a criticism. Many people don't realize that we stereotype all the time, often completely unintentionally. Stereotyping is actually a rather efficient process which allows us to 'know' a lot of things about something without ever having seen it before.

To understand this simply, think about the first time you get into a new car. When you buy it, you can immediately get into it and drive it away. How can you do this? Of course, it is because you have certain information stored in your head about cars. You know how to open the door to get into it, fasten your seatbelt, turn on the ignition, remove the handbrake, engage the correct gear, and drive away. All of this information is stored in your head, based on your previous experience with cars. You don't need to start from scratch and work everything out about that particular car.

This particular aspect of the information stored in your head about types of thing that you encounter in everyday life is known as a *schema*. You have schemas about all sorts of objects that allow you to recognize the object with just a few pieces of information about it, and then apply all the stored knowledge that you have about that category of object. For the car, this will be stored in your 'car' schema. Therefore, as soon as you have recognized the new object as a car, you already know lots of things about it. All of the additional information which makes it different from your last car – perhaps it's a manual instead of an automatic, or a 5 door instead of a 3 door – you can apply separately, but the fundamentals of 'a car' remain the same.

Looked at in this way, you can see that this is actually quite an effective way to process information. Given that we cannot process everything that our brains take in, it makes sense to be able to draw on stored information, in order to speed up the process by which we recognize and react to an object. Imagine if you had to learn absolutely everything about every new object that you encountered in everyday life. Simple tasks like opening doors and making cups of coffee would have to be worked out each time we did them. Schematic processing is very efficient.

Humans have different types of schema for different types of information. For example, we have person schemas, which store information about different types of people and how we expect them to behave. We have role schemas about the different roles that people carry out in life, and these contain expectations about what we expect from people in those roles – for example, we might expect a nurse to be caring, a mother to be maternal, and a teacher to be knowledgeable. We have event schemas, which tell us about what might happen in certain social activities and situations, which contain information about how we should behave and how others should behave. Every time we encounter a person or a situation, our minds apply the information that we hold in our schemas, and set up an expectation of what might happen.

Schemas contain knowledge of general characteristics, but leave room for variations in each situation – as with the new car. Therefore, you are actually adding to them all the time, as you encounter people and situations, and get new information to compile in your schema. Schemas can cover all sorts of things that affect you in everyday life – types of people, different places, different activities, different social situations. You will have schemas for all of the issues that you feel strongly about, either positively or negatively.

These schemas are applied to everything in your life! That's not something that you can do much about, it is a basic functioning mechanism of the human brain. However, you can do something about the content of your schemas, once you start to understand what's in them. If you want to know the content, start thinking about some of the things mentioned above. What do you believe about them?

Let's take parties as an example. If you're a very sociable, popular person, you might think that parties are huge fun. If you hate having to socialize and find it difficult to make friends, you might think parties are a form of social torture and avoid them where possible! You will have information in your 'party' schema which will tell you all about parties – how you should act, how other people should act, and what you expect to happen. The 'party' schemas of the two types of person mentioned above would look very different – even if they had attended the very same parties throughout their lives.

When you understand this, you will begin to see how much effect the information stored inside your head has on your view of the world around you. Like all the information stored in the mind, the information stored in schemas is open to be changed – but we don't always realize what's in there and how it might hold us back.

The basic process going on inside your head which produces schemas is called *categorization*. Exactly as it says, you put things and people into categories inside your head, based on your judgment about which category they belong to. The way in which this process works automatically makes us exaggerate the similarities within categories, and the differences between them. This can lead to problems which you may not be aware of.

For example, you may have a schema for 'rich people', in which you store all of the information that you believe to apply to them. You may see them as snobbish, and as looking down on anyone who does not fit into the 'rich people' schema. If so, you may meet a rich person and automatically assume that he will be a snob and will look down on you, before he has even opened his mouth! You don't know anything about this person other than that they are rich, but the way that the brain functions will immediately apply all of the information in your schema. This will influence the way that you react, and the way that you respond to this person – which will in turn affect the way that he responds to you. If you think a lot of people are looking down their noses at you, you may want to look at your own expectations about how people behave.

The other aspect of this which you need to consider is how the information that you hold in your schemas affects you. Think back again to your 'rich person' schema. Do you think rich people are happy, relaxed and generous, or do you think they are work-obsessed, stressed and mean with their money? If your schema contains the second type of information, and you want to be rich yourself, take a moment to think how that might work in your head. Effectively, you are telling yourself to become something that you don't like very much. Why would anyone do to that? If you're consciously saying that you want to be rich, but subconsciously believe that rich people are unpleasant, then subconsciously you will keep sabotaging yourself, because why would you want to be something that you believe to be unpleasant?

Schemas are socially produced things – they are built up from the information that you receive from the people around you and the things that you experience in your interactions with the world. In fact, schemas would not work if they weren't social, they rely on information being shared. We've already seen that they can be a good thing, because they make it easier for you to process information efficiently. However, they can also be a bad thing, and can lead to stereotyping of the kind mentioned in the first paragraph of this chapter – because they can lead to biases and distortions. When you are using preconceptions, you will automatically have some information that is 'wrong'. All people, and all situations, are individual. Although you do have the ability to make variations for each person and situation, you may not get round to applying that if you have already made a judgment based on your schema information.

The other issue here is that schemas are self-confirming. Think about the 'rich person' example mentioned above. If you meet this man, and he sees that you are looking at him in an unfriendly manner, he may turn away from you and go to speak to someone who looks a little less hostile. This may be purely because he thinks that you don't want to speak to him, but of course you might not realize that – you will interpret it as evidence that rich people are snobs and that he does not want to speak to you because he is looking down on you – and this will further reinforce the information that you have in your schema about rich people being unpleasant snobs.

This brings us on to *attribution*. Humans invariably assign reasons for behavior to people. In this case you would have assigned the reason for behavior to snobbishness, whereas the real reason might be a desire to speak only to friendly people! Attributions are a very important part of the human experience; we are fairly unique in our desire to understand *why* people behave as they do, and to feel the need to understand it. The causes that we attribute to behavior can be either internal (down to the person themselves) or external (due to outside influence). The schema information that we hold about that 'type' of person will influence whether we see their behavior as being motivated by internal or external forces.

Imagine that you are a teacher, and one of your students has failed an important test. What might you attribute this to? The answer, of course, depends on your view of the student. If they are generally uninterested in your subject and don't try very hard, you will probably attribute the failure to not paying attention in class, no revision being done, and a lack of aptitude for the subject. If this was the result of the best student in your class, you might attribute it to illness or problems at home, or even worry that you did not give your students the correct amount of teaching on the subject matter of the test.

Studies have found that, in general, we are more likely to attribute internal causes for other people, and external causes for ourselves! This of course is influenced by the information that we hold in our schema about that person, and whether we can explain events in line with the schema. In the example above, it would be easy to attribute internal causes for the first student, as they are in line with our perceptions about her. If we believe her to by lazy and disinterested, it's simple enough to assume that the test failure was down to lack of effort. For the second student, this is more challenging, so the teacher might turn to external attributions to try to explain it. Of course, the teacher might be wrong in both cases! The first student may have decided to put in a huge amount of effort to improve her results in the subject, but been ill on the day and made a mess of the test. The second student might have decided that she was going to drop the subject anyway, and therefore not bothered to put in the time on it. The important thing to understand about attributions is that we make the best ones that we can, based on the information that we have and the underlying processes of the brain, but they are not always right! They are, in effect, an educated guess, unless we have evidence to prove them as factual.

As I mentioned above, we also make attributions for our own behavior and results, and in general we are more inclined to believe these to be external. This does change depending on whether we consider the behavior or result to be good or bad! For example, someone whose business has been hugely successful might attribute the cause to hard work, knowledge of her subject and clever identification of a niche in the market. Someone whose business had failed might cite the reasons as market conditions or an untrustworthy business partner. The reasons that we do this are believed to be two-fold. Firstly, most of us don't do something when we already have an expectation that we won't succeed at it – therefore, when we fail, we attribute the failure to external causes. Secondly, it's motivational, and acts to raise our self-esteem. Interestingly, people with high self-esteem have been proved to do this more than others, but we don't yet know if they do this *because* of their higher self-esteem, or if self-esteem is higher as a result!

The other factor which needs to be taken into consideration here is known as *Theory of Mind*. This is the ability of humans to try to put themselves in another person's position and to try to understand how they would be thinking and feeling. The ability to do this is certainly not equal among all humans. Some people find it very difficult to put themselves into someone else's situation – indeed, some people do not even try! Even where you do try, you will be biased by the schema information that you hold about that person. It is very hard for us as humans to be totally objective. For instance, if you believe that door-to-door salesmen are all conmen who just want to rip you off, you will find it hard to believe that the man standing in your doorstep is genuinely enthusiastic about the product he's trying to sell you – you will believe that he is just interested in making a quick profit, and there's a good chance you won't listen to him. It is worth noting that we are more likely to go outside the basic information that we hold in our schemas if the person or thing is important to us – so if the item being sold is something that you have really wanted but could not afford, and it's being offered at half the price that it's selling for in the shops, there's a good chance that you would dismiss the schema information which was suggesting you would be ripped off, and listen to the salesman!

The above point is important because it confirms that we can ignore schema information when it's in our interests to do so. This suggests the ability to be able to rise above our schema information where it is holding us back from something we want. We stereotype ourselves in exactly the same way as we stereotype others – with the slight variance that we try to shift things to our advantage in explaining our relative successes and failures in the world (and we do this with others that we care about or sympathize with too, as you will know if you often find yourself making excuses for people!)

Think about the ways in which you do this. For a start, think about the groups into which you put yourself. Now take one as an example. 'Mum' is a good one. If you have put yourself into the group 'Mum', you will have an idea of the behaviors that you expect a good mother should have. For example, some women think that it's wrong to go back to work when you have children unless you absolutely have to. If you believe this, then it's likely that you would not go back to work. Some people think that there's nothing wrong with mums going back to work, but that they should always spend time with their kids in the evening. These mums are also following their own idea of how a mum should behave, and they don't feel they are not being a good mum by going back to work. Point 1 – stereotypes are not only generalizations, they are subjective generalizations! The rules for your categories are your own rules, they will not be identical to someone else's rules for that category.

Point 2 – as we get older and we change and develop as a person, we also change the categories that we put ourselves in. Having done so, we then adopt what we consider to be the 'correct' beliefs and behaviors for that group. Wanting to fit in is a natural desire – from the motivation of certain animals to be part of a herd for the protection that this gives from predators, to the complex human emotional desires to fit in and to be accepted. Even those who think that they don't want to fit in, when thinking about it deeply, will realize that they have put themselves in a 'misfits' group and are probably behaving accordingly!

Given that we do this subconsciously, does it not make sense to use it to our advantage? You can change the groups that you see yourself belonging to, and the way that you stereotype yourself. What you are today does not have to be the same as what you will be tomorrow. You have been changing all of your life, to a greater or lesser degree. If you consciously take control of your own thoughts, your own beliefs about yourself and others, and about your ability to create the things in life that you desire, you will find that your attitudes and behaviors will automatically change in line with your new beliefs. Take a close look at the things that you believe about yourself and about other people, the schemas that you have put yourself in and your beliefs about them. What is helping you? What is holding you back?

Now that you understand how conditioning and stereotyping have helped to shape you into the person that you are today, let's move on to looking at beliefs and how they affect us in everyday life.

8 BELIEFS, EMOTIONS AND ATTITUDES

Now that we have looked at how our experienced reality is made up from our beliefs, and how our beliefs are built up through processes such as conditioning and stereotyping, we can start to take a closer look at our own individual, personal beliefs, how they influence our choices and decisions, and how they are such a fundamental part of what we are. If you change your programming, your beliefs, stereotypes and conditioning, you will change both the person that you are now, and the person that you can become. We will also look at the effect that our emotions have on our lives, and how these combine with beliefs to produce the person that we become and the things that we do.

BELIEFS
Remember, none of the things which we believe about ourselves are a true reality. If they are holding us back, we can and must change them. You got to the place you are at now with the beliefs that you currently hold. To become something better, happier, and more fulfilled, your

beliefs must change, or no matter how much effort you put into moving forward, you can only end up in the same place.

To begin to make a change, we need to understand what beliefs are helping, and what beliefs are holding us back. No matter who you are, you will have some beliefs that are supportive and some beliefs that are hindering. Go back to chapter 1, and look again at what you wrote down about your characteristics and skills. Which of those do you find positive? Which are negative? Which are not in line with the person that you want to be?

All of these things that you listed are contained in your schema of yourself. Like all schemas, the information in it is built up from past knowledge and experience. As we discussed in the last chapter, schemas are social – so the background you grew up in and the people who surround you will all contribute to the information in the schema labeled 'Me'.

It's not as simple as this, of course. As we said earlier, everything is a product of biopsychosocial influence. Therefore, it's just not possible to assume that if you had a happy childhood and supportive parents, you will be a success in life; and if you had an unhappy childhood and unsupportive parents, you will be a failure. If you look at the world around you, you'll find plenty of people who grew up in a very affluent environment who have failed to achieve the things they wanted from life; conversely, you will find a number of people who grew up in very difficult environments who have achieved enormous fame and fortune.

Early advantages do not guarantee success, and early disadvantages do not rule it out. It may be easier to get on if you have advantages in early life, but this is mostly down to social skills, academic knowledge and self-confidence that can be learned at any time. I was lucky enough to go to boarding school, and to learn these skills at an early age, and I can honestly tell you that these are learned social skills, and learned states of mind, which come automatically with practice over the years. Like anything else, if you do it enough, it becomes second nature.

You must bear in mind too that not only the social environment influences us. We also have individual cognitive processes and individual genetic make-up. You will have seen yourself that some people are generally happy and cheerful, and others miserable and withdrawn. If you have genetics and thought processes that always see everything in the worst possible light, the good news is that you can change them (in fact, we will look at how to change all three of these areas in later chapters) and – as they all influence each other – how improving any one will have a positive impact in all areas. The bad news is that if you are a generally dissatisfied person who never takes any pleasure in any of their achievements, getting your next promotion or starting your next project is not going to be enough for you. The problem isn't with your achievements, it's with your programming. For some people, any level of success is never enough. If you don't stop to take pleasure in, and perhaps don't even acknowledge, your achievements, nothing that you do will ever change that. We'll look at this later, too. There is always hope. Now that you are starting to understand how your mind works, you will begin to see how you can change it – whatever the basis of your problems.

When you start to examine your beliefs at this level, understanding how you have acquired them, you begin to see how everything in your past and present comes together to shape the person that you are now.

Look back at your programming, in terms of your beliefs and your schemas. Why might you not feel able to do the things that you want to do? Perhaps classical conditioning has taught you to associate that thing with something negative, and subconsciously you are fighting against it, though you may not be aware of it.

Think back to the example of meeting a rich person

which we looked at in the last chapter. If the information in your schema about rich people tells you that they are not very nice, you can see where you might have problems. If you heard all through your childhood that rich people are awful, you will have *learned* that being rich means being awful, and why would you want to be awful? Of course, being rich (or being poor) doesn't make you awful – being awful makes you awful! – but if your programming has taught you that, and your schema has stored it, you have accepted it as a belief, and at a subconscious level you will fight against it.

The same will be true if you believe rich people are overworked and die of heart attacks in their fifties – or if you believe that they don't have real friends, just those who want to get things from them – or if you believe they lose all of their friends as they gain their money. If your health and your friends matter to you, you will subconsciously reject money, in order to keep your health and your friends, because your beliefs will tell you that you cannot have both.

Another example: being attractive. Attractiveness is also subjective, but from experience, if you ask most people, they would say that they would like to be attractive. A lot of people I speak to are dissatisfied with their looks. When you first think about this, it seems quite obvious: why would you not want to be attractive?

Now consider what your programming may have taught you about this, in terms of your beliefs and your schemas. If you're female, what does your schema say about attractive women? If you were the school nerd, who was bullied by the 'popular' girls, it might tell you that attractive women are spiteful and vindictive. Programming may have taught you to associate being beautiful with being nasty to those less fortunate in the looks department. Again, if you don't want to be spiteful and nasty, if you believe this, would you want to be attractive? However much you believe you want to be, your subconscious will be steering you away from becoming one of the mean girls from school, and sabotaging your efforts.

The point here is that it does not matter what logic says. You can think you want to be rich, famous, successful, popular and gorgeous all you like – if your subconscious programming is telling you that these are negative things to be, it will sabotage your success in these areas. That's part of its job, after all – it learns through programming, and uses that programming to guide you. It's full of the rules and information that you have programmed into it yourself, and that you have let others program into it.

IF YOUR SUBCONSCIOUS IS NOT ALIGNED WITH YOUR CONSCIOUS DESIRES, IT WILL OVERRIDE THEM.

If you're saying that you're a logical person who would never let a lot of mental brainwashing override their conscious goals and plans, you need to rethink that. Years ago, I was also a non-believer in the power of the subconscious. I disliked the idea that my brain would not do exactly what I told it to do, and was sure that logic and intellect could solve every problem. What I found was that I was perfectly capable of starting things and doing well in them, but after a period of time I would get bored with them, start to dislike them, and not want to do them any more. As soon as anything started to go well for me, I would find a really good reason to stop doing it.

There were two problems in my life that were well beyond my conscious knowledge at the time to understand. The first was that I was angry and rebellious, and being successful didn't fit in with that well at all. Subconsciously, I was hanging onto the things that I felt angry and rebellious about, and if everything was going right, I would not have that any more. My belief was that life was unfair, and my subconscious did its best to prove that for me. Beliefs are a self-fulfilling prophecy, and your subconscious will do all it can to materialize them for you! Secondly, I was doing the things that my schemas were telling me I was expected to do, not the things that I wanted to do. That gave me something else to be angry and rebellious about, I was a master of self-sabotage. My life was a constant battle between my conscious mind, which was well-educated and resourceful and capable of doing many things, and my subconscious, which wanted to make my beliefs a reality for me.

Think of your subconscious like a computer. It doesn't care if the things you have in it are good or bad, it just processes them and gives you an output. You can have the best computer software in the world (your conscious mind) but if the data it's processing is bad, you'll get bad results. You need to change the data – your beliefs. Before you can change it, you need to understand what's in that data – which is why it's so important to be able to analyze the beliefs that you are holding, understand where they came from, and challenge them if they are not helping you.

EMOTIONS

Emotions are another product of your subconscious, and again they are biopsychosocial. This means that all of the emotions you experience will depend on your biology, your thought processes, and the social environment around you.

If you are one of those people who says "Other people make me angry/unhappy/depressed", think again. Your mind makes you angry, unhappy or depressed (or happy, motivated and positive!) – it has a lot of chemicals (called neurotransmitters) that it deploys for precisely that purpose. Other people have an input and an influence, and your conscious mind has the ability to stop and steer that emotion if you want it to, but never be under the impression that anyone can MAKE your mind do anything.

PEOPLE ONLY HAVE THE POWER OVER YOU THAT YOU GIVE TO THEM.

I want you to stop for a moment and think about that, because in my experience, most people give others an awful lot of power over them, and believe that they have no choice in the matter. The truth is that there is always a choice. We can't control the things that people do to us (although if the people around us do bad things a lot of the time, we might want to change the people we are associating with!) but we can always, always control the reaction that we make to it. This is one of the greatest powers that you have, and one of the things that can make the most difference to your life.

Think for a moment about how you react if someone does something hurtful to you. Say someone that you thought was a friend is found to be spreading nasty, untrue gossip about you. How do you react?

Probably, you would react with anger and hurt. These are pretty normal emotions to experience when someone you trusted lets you down. At this stage, you have two choices. You can dwell on and nurture these emotions and they will make you miserable. If you dwell on them too much, they might even make you ill. Or, you can make a choice to accept that this is how you felt, take control of your emotions, and move on.

This may sound simple; I know that it isn't. In what was undoubtedly the worst experience of my life, someone that I trusted, a family member, did something awful to me with no provocation whatsoever. This person, whom I had always done my best to help, almost ruined my life. I put my business on hold, lay about the house without the motivation to do anything, started eating lots of junk, and was generally a total mess. This went on for months, while I tried to put right the havoc that she had caused to me and my loved ones. That was the only thing I had any motivation to do; my life was totally on hold.

Even when I had put right everything that she had done, I did not feel the same as I had done before. All of the energy which had once gone into my family, my interests, my businesses and my investments was now totally focused on her. I was eaten up by my anger, and unhappy because I could not understand how someone I had shown nothing but kindness could try to destroy my life.

There is a quote, by persons unknown, which says 'To hold onto anger is like drinking poison and expecting the other person to die".

You need to understand this: hating that person did not hurt her at all. She didn't even experience it, because we did not see her any more. The only person it hurt was me.

I had just started studying NLP at that time, and I really did not understand what the books meant when they said that we should forgive people. As far as my conscious mind was concerned, what she had done was calculated, malicious and completely unforgiveable. I was missing the point, and so are you, if you think that you are forgiving for the benefit of the person that has hurt you. What you need to do is let go of it, and the person that benefits is you.

I am not suggesting for a minute that you rush up to someone who has deliberately hurt you, throw your arms round them and tell them that you forgive them. If someone has set out to hurt you, and they show no signs of remorse for it, then why would you want that person around you? However, spending energy that you could better focus on the things you want and the people you love on hating someone is not sensible.

If your head is full of negative emotions all the time, it's not possible for you to be positive, motivated and focused on good things. The fact that your anger may be justified is irrelevant.

The point is, it's bad for you. What's better – to hold onto justifiable anger, or to reject your right to be angry, decide to be happy, and decide that person isn't going to impact your life any more? This is *your* choice – and the person who hurt you does not have the power to make you stay feeling unhappy if you don't let them.

We have the power to control our emotions far more than we realize. Emotions are a subconscious response to our biopsychosocial experience. Some people are far more easily able to control them than others. Some people are naturally disposed, by genetics, thought processes and experience, to shrug off negative emotions and focus on the things that they want in their lives. Some are not. Believe me, I was not born with this skill. I have learned it, because I came to realize over the course of studying and experimenting that it was absolutely essential if I wanted to achieve my goals.

We don't yet know exactly how the processes that work in our brains tie back to the emotions that we experience, but we do know that both the brain's chemistry and physical connections are activated by emotion, and that we can change our emotions by applying different thought processes. We'll look at how this is done later in the book. For now, it's enough to understand that our emotions and our beliefs combine to produce our attitudes to life, and that these attitudes strongly influence our behaviors.

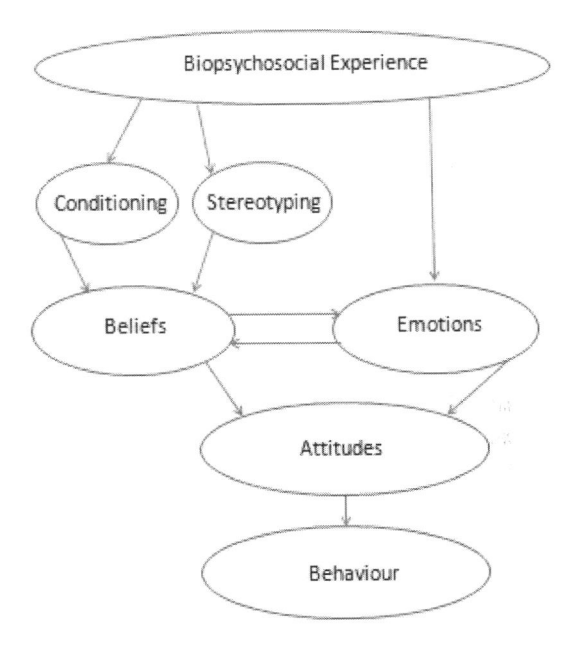

```
                    Biopsychosocial Experience
                    /        |           \
          Conditioning   Stereotyping     |
                \        /                |
                 Beliefs  ⇌  Emotions
                       \      /
                       Attitudes
                          |
                       Behaviour
```

The image above sums up what we've looked at over the last few chapters. Your experience, which is defined by your biological, cognitive and social parameters, feeds into the things that you experience in your day to day living, to build up your conditioning and stereotypes, and to form your belief system, which contains beliefs both about yourself and about other people and things. It also feeds into the emotions that you experience. Your beliefs and your emotions form your attitudes to life, which in turn will define how you respond to any given situation.

In order to change your beliefs, you need to understand your conditioning and your stereotyping and change that which is not beneficial to the things that you want in life. To change both your beliefs and your emotional responses, you need to take conscious control of your psychosocial experience. If your emotional responses and your beliefs change, your attitude will change automatically.

ATTITUDES

Think about this. Imagine that you've been out of work for a while, and have started to feel generally demoralized. You believe that you're not capable of succeeding in life, in whatever area you want to succeed in, and you feel generally depressed and demotivated. What will your attitude be if you are offered an interview for a job that you would really like?

Now imagine that you're in the same position, but have refused to let it get you down. You view your current situation as a temporary setback. You realize that you have a lot to offer a company, and are sure that when the right position comes up, an employer will realize how much you could bring to his business. You are looking forward to getting the opportunity to put this unfortunate period of your life behind you and get back on with your career. You get the same letter offering you an interview for a really good job. How will you feel?

You need to understand that what you feel will show through to your prospective employer. What you feel on the inside is reflected on the outside. If you go into that interview with the first attitude, feeling you're not much use and why would anyone want to give you a good job, what do you think will happen? If you were interviewing for a new staff member, and you had to choose between someone who gave hesitant, unenthusiastic answers, and someone who had taken the trouble to find out about the company, spoke confidently about the role, and showed a high level of enthusiasm, who do you think you would offer the job to? The truth is, the first person might be even more anxious to get the job (as he won't be so confident that another will come along any day if he doesn't get this one) and he might be equally as qualified as the second person. He might even do the job better! But if he doesn't get chance to prove that, the employer will never find it out; and if he doesn't come across with the right attitude, chances are that he won't get the job.

This applies across life. Imagine that you had to choose a doctor to carry out an important operation for you. Would you choose the doctor who confidently told you about all the similar operations he had carried out, and his high success rate, or the one who appeared nervous and not really engaged with what he was doing?

Your attitudes will define how you respond to the things that life throws at you. Different people cope in different ways with challenges, setbacks and disappointments. Their reactions are governed by their attitudes, and their attitudes are governed by their beliefs and emotions. Following back through the diagram above, at the very top level we get back once again to the biopsychosocial influences. This is where you need to focus your attention, assert control, and make your changes. With the understanding of your past programming and your schemas, you can then challenge unhelpful data. You can also set yourself up to set off an alert when you experience any emotions which are not helpful. You will find that your attitudes then begin to change, and that your behavior will change naturally as a result of this.

Before we move on to look at making these changes, I have included a couple of chapters around personality and identity. I have realized while speaking to people about the topics we have discussed in this book that many of people's issues with making changes are that they believe it is somehow a challenge to who they are. In the next two chapters we will look more closely at personality and identity formation, and how these can be viewed in such a way as to be either a help or a hindrance to you.

9 PERSONALITY VS. IDENTITY

In this chapter we will look at the meanings of personality and identity, their similarities and their differences.

Whether we are aware of it or not, we all have a number of identities in our lives, usually correlating to our interests and the roles that we play. For instance, under my identities, I might list wife, mother, business owner, coach, project manager. Please note that by "identities" I do not mean personalities. You don't need multiple personalities! (In fact, psychology will tell you that fragmented personality is a sign of mental ill-health).

Your core personality underlies everything that you do. It is, essentially, you – the type of person you are, how you interact with people, how you deal with life. We will look at personality in more detail in the next chapter. For now though, be aware that it's there, and it's a single entity, no matter how many identities you overlay on top of it.

So why do we need identities, how are they useful, and how can they be used to our benefit?

We've said that identities are effectively roles that we play in life. The main benefit of this is that it helps us to segregate the different skills that we need for different areas in our lives. You need very different qualities for very different roles. It can help to understand that having to use these skills in one area of our lives does not mean that we have to bring them into other areas, although we can do so if they are useful there. Having a role where you use certain identity traits does not mean that these have to become part of your core personality.

For instance, imagine that you are an officer aboard a naval ship. One of your duties is to make sure that the men serving under you are smart, efficient and well-trained. The skills that you bring to this job will involve management and organization. You will want to make sure that everything is regimented, well organized and done very precisely. These are the skills that make you good at your job.

Now imagine that you're at home on shore leave. How useful are these skills? You could argue that management and organization are useful to have in any area of life, but there are limits to how far you can usefully apply them. If you find yourself lining up the children for drill and uniform inspection, and yelling at them because they have a mark on their shirt, it might not be so successful. Your wife is probably not going to appreciate it if you start ordering her about, setting her task lists, and checking on everything after she's done it.

If you're a racing driver, doing something that requires immense focus and concentration, do you think you might find it hard to switch off and relax when you come home? How about if you're a stock market trader? Many people find it difficult to leave their 'work' persona in the office when they come home. For some people, for example some highly successful business people, there may be no 'home' – their business might make demands on them in the way of ideas, planning, or clients or partners calling seven days a week, at any time of the day or night, if they allow it to do so.

Again, this is not to say that some of the qualities you

use in each of these roles could not be helpful in other areas of your life, but be aware of two things.

Firstly, you do not need to define yourself by any of these traits. They may be a part of your core personality, they may not.

Secondly, you can use your identities to get to the places that you want to be. You just need to make sure that you have the right identity for the right role.

I know that some people have issues understanding this. For those who play role-playing games online, let me steal an example from that. Within the game, you have a character that you play. The basic nature of the character does not change, but you will have 'traits' that you can swap in and out on that character, as and when you need them. For different tasks, different traits will be beneficial. When you don't need those traits, and something else would be more useful, you swap them out. They are always there, available for use as and when you need them, but you don't always have them slotted on your character.

Identities and traits work in much the same way, except that, unlike in a game, you don't have a finite number of slots that you can use! You are limited only by your imagination and ability to put yourself into that mode, as to the number of useful traits that you can call upon.

You might draw the relationship between personality and identities like this:

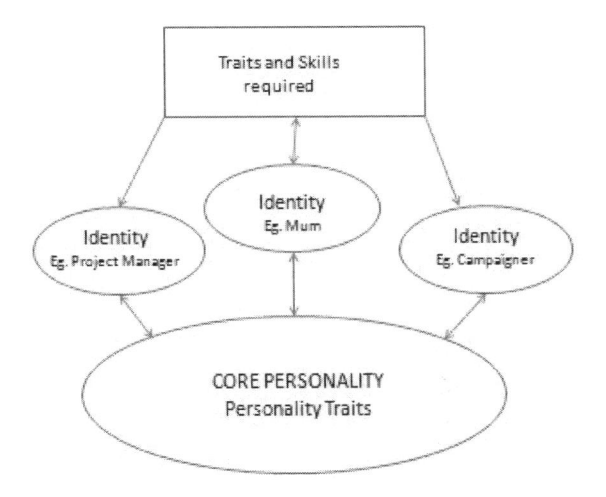

[Diagram: "Traits and Skills required" box at top, connected by arrows to three "Identity" ovals (Eg. Project Manager, Eg. Mum, Eg. Campaigner), which connect to a large "CORE PERSONALITY – Personality Traits" oval at the bottom.]

So, as the picture demonstrates, you have a central, core personality, and separately to this, you have a number of identities relating to the roles that you take in your life.

Some traits may be common to all identities, and you will usually find that these form part of your core personality. It's very important to me that I should be polite to everyone, and this trait appears no matter what role I may be taking on at the time. It's a core personality trait. Other traits may emerge in only one identity, because they may only be helpful in that one particular role.

A useful thing to remember is that identity can be used to build and work on traits. A trait such as self-confidence could be built up within an identity (such as being effective in your job, whatever that may be) and integrated into core personality as it grows. This is why setbacks in one area of our life have such a big impact on others. Confidence, for example, can be gained or built in one role, which has an effect on your core personality and filters through to the other identities.

Some traits are inherently unhelpful. For instance, if you are naturally despondent, you may find this of very limited use to you. Some traits may initially appear negative, but they can actually be useful in certain situations. For example, being pessimistic may get in the way of some of the things that you want to do, but can urge you to caution which can prevent you making costly mistakes. Blind optimism is not a good thing. Being demotivated may initially seem to be a hindrance, but what if it's your body telling you that it's worn out and you need to take it easier for a while?

Learn to recognize the traits that you have, and identify the traits that you need. You may need to acquire assertiveness or confidence. Which traits are you lacking in that you need to consciously work on? What traits do you have that are unhelpful, that you might need to consciously suppress?

Be aware that some things in your core personality may cause problems in your identities. If you are a naturally shy person, and the roles that you carry out require you to be assertive, you will find that you are constantly having to battle against your natural inclinations. In this situation, you have two choices – work on your shyness, or concede that you are not going to be able to do the roles that you want to do without a feeling of discomfort.

You will also find that some things in your identities can cause problems in your core personality. Imagine you have taken on a sales job with a company that has fairly aggressive marketing techniques. If you're a very ethical person, and you feel that hard sell is bad practice, how can you be happy doing a job which is constantly going to force you to go against your ethics? Being ethical is a core personality trait which most people would not want to lose. It would be sensible in this situation to accept that you are never going to be a ruthless commission earner, and find a role that does not go against your core values.

If you think that identities are a strange concept, think

again. You are using them all the time, maybe without being aware of it. We construct and reconstruct ourselves continually, based on the situations we encounter in life and our interactions with other people.

You are not a fixed person. It's very unlikely that you are the same person now that you were ten years ago, and very unlikely that you will be the same person in ten years' time. We grow through our interactions, and we have the ability to constantly learn. It's a misconception that personality and identity are fixed by the end of childhood, although change does slow down in most people unless they make a conscious effort to keep changing and growing. You are not constrained either by your past or present circumstances to keep the situation in life that you have now.

Not only do we constantly reconstruct ourselves, we naturally construct ourselves in different ways for different circumstances. We do this through conversation, both with others and with ourselves. In all of our interactions with others, we build ourselves into the image of the person we feel we should be in that role. It's like an ongoing story that continues throughout our lives, with ourselves as the authors.

Given that we do this naturally, does it not make sense to use this to our advantage?

Let me give you an example. Do you remember that I said the motivation for this book began because people frequently asked me how I do what I do? Here is the basic strategy for doing that.

Firstly, you need to understand what it is that you want to do, or to be. You also need to make sure that you really want it. Picture yourself in the role – really try to feel it. When you think about being in this role, if you feel a sense of excitement and anticipation, that's a good sign. If you think about the role and feel nervous or uncomfortable, or unenthusiastic, that's a bad sign. If you think this is totally obvious, look around you at all the people doing jobs that they hate. Sometimes they studied for years to qualify for this job. It's not as obvious as you might think.

If you feel comfortable when you think about being in the role, set a goal to get there. This must be sincere and fully committed. Saying you 'want to be' something is not enough. Saying you WILL be something, and are prepared to do what it takes to get there, is something very different.

Now that you have made that decision and commitment, you need more information. The best way to get this is to model someone who is already doing what you want to do – if it's not someone you know, it might be someone famous. If you don't have a model, the Internet is a great research tool. What does that person know? How do they speak, dress, act towards others? How do they think? How do they meet challenges? Are there courses that they would need to have studied, qualifications that they would need to have?

Now, most importantly, you need to FEEL it. How would YOU feel in that role? What would you look like, speak like, think like? What would be different to how you are now? More knowledge? More confidence? Something else?

We will look at these techniques more thoroughly later in the book, but first I'm going to take you through a closer look at your personality, because it's critical to understand the person you are before you start trying to forge the person you want to be.

10 PERSONALITY

The power in controlling your mind starts to become apparent when you begin to combine all of the information in the previous chapters and apply them in your life. Now that you have an understanding of beliefs, programming and identities, you can begin to look at how this affects your core personality, and to identify the things that are holding you back.

Earlier in the book, you wrote down your perspective on the traits that you have. If you have defined your personality in the past, it was most likely in light of your views on these traits. After reading this far, you will understand that these are actually beliefs that you have about yourself, and that some of them may be true, and some of them may be the result of past programming and self-stereotyping. All of them will be a combination of your genetics, your thought processes and your social conditioning. Once you know this, you can begin to look at your traits in a different light, and start to make the changes that you want.

Let's start by looking at this at a high level. Overall, do you like yourself as a person? Are you the sort of person that people want to be around? Do you inspire those around you, or do you make them feel bad about themselves? How do people see you?

Bear in mind that people can only go by what you put out into the world. If you're manifesting unhappiness, anger or impatience, this is what those around you will pick up on. If you think that you're really a nice person but people can't see that, then you're a victim of your own projections. Many of us are stressed and dissatisfied with life and take it out on those around us, all the time thinking that people should see the true character beneath the manifestations of negative emotion. Unfortunately, this isn't going to happen. Very few people in your life will know you well enough to see the 'real' you if that isn't what you're putting out there.

Would *you* like to be around you?

If you're reading this book, and you've got this far through it, the chances are that you want to make an improvement in your life and you're serious about making the changes that are needed. If this is so, bear in mind that our relationships with other people are an absolutely key part of the human experience, and that the quality of our relationships, whether they are in the home, at work, or social, materially alters our enjoyment of life, and how we get on in the world. I appreciate that it can be difficult if you have a roadblock in your life and are feeling resentful and frustrated, but you really do need to make the effort not to allow this to control your life. Taking things out on the people around you may be a natural human reaction, but it doesn't help you move forward, and it does not contribute to your happiness.

Remember also that you will have modeled what you saw as a child – or you may have anti-modeled it! If your mum or dad came home from work totally stressed and shouted at the children, you may have learned that this is the correct way to respond – or alternatively, you may have disliked being shouted at so much that you decided never to yell at your own children because you had a problem at work. Even in our modeling, we have a choice.

Statistics say that the majority of people who were beaten as children beat their own kids. This may be true, but there are many people who had a violent upbringing who reacted by becoming extremely anti-violence and would never hit their own family members, because they know what it feels like to have been on the receiving end; they would never inflict that unhappiness on their own family. You have a choice – and you go on having choices throughout life. If you have made wrong choices, there's no reason why you can't make a better one now. Your modeling shapes you, but it can only control you if you let it.

Modeling plays a great part in the extent to which we are programmed as children, affecting our confidence, emotional responses and reactions. Think back now to your childhood, and the people that influenced you at that time.

Do you remember having a hero? If you thought very highly of someone – maybe a parent, aunt or uncle, older sibling or neighbor's child – there is a good chance that subconsciously you modeled their views, actions and opinions. Our thoughts are not all our own, as we cannot learn independently of our environment. If you have very deep-seated beliefs about something, can you remember a role model from whom you might have taken in these ideas? Conversely, if you are very against something, can you think of a person whose ideas or behavior you did not like?

The problem with this is that you can take on other people's opinions as to what makes you a success as a person. These are what have been called your 'conditions of worth'. If the conditions of worth that have been imposed on you are not in line with your own desires and values, this can cause immense amounts of problems in your life, as you struggle to be someone that you are not, in order to fulfill someone else's requirements.

One of the things that you need to be able to do is to assess your own dreams and ambitions, and make sure that they really are the things that you want. This is called 'congruence'. If you're incongruent, then you are fighting a losing battle because you don't really have motivation to achieve the things that you think you desire. You also may be trying to cultivate personality traits that you don't really want to have.

Imagine someone with a parent who owned an economically successful but ecologically unfriendly business. If that person at heart is a passionate environmentalist, but has taken on a goal of running and improving the business because their parent has made them believe this is the 'correct' dream, they will have a huge issue with incongruence. Modeling continues throughout life, and you may still be modeling people you should not be. Who have you modeled in the past? Who are you modeling now? Is what you are modeling congruent with what you really want?

We have various defense mechanisms which allow us to deal with things that we cannot cope with, and these work subconsciously. Therefore, you may not be aware of them. For example, we can transfer emotions that we feel about one person onto another person, if we find it easier to cope that way. You can be angry with your husband because you're angry with your dad, or your boss. You can transfer the passion that you feel for one thing into something else, because you feel the first thing is not right or possible. There are a number of different techniques that we subconsciously use, so for every dream and goal and emotion you have, ask yourself why it's important to you. Is this what you really want, or feel?

Understand yourself, understand your motivations, and learn to assess whether they truly are *your* motivations. Don't waste your energy on something that you don't really want.

The other thing to be aware of is that being too tough

on yourself is not helpful to you. Many of us can be pretty hard on ourselves, and take the things that we do and achieve in life as a measure of our worth and our success as a person. Be very careful as to how you define yourself. There are many ways of looking at things, and quite often we choose negative ones. The way that we portray ourselves, that we tell our own story, is enormously important. Without changing a single actual thing in your life, you can change your whole outlook and perception. We do this by challenging our negative responses, and framing our perceptions into something more positive. Remember, perceptions are not the truth – they are filtered end products of our senses, cognitive processes and stored information.

If you're saying that there are some things that just don't have a positive side, you're right. Does that mean that you have to look at them in the worst possible light, and that you can't try to change your perspective? Absolutely not.

You might say 'I am stressed!' This could be read as, I am a stressful person. That's not actually correct. Stress is something that you are experiencing but it's not *you* (and even if you do this all the time, it's still not you, it's an unhelpful way that you have learned to react to a difficult situation – remember that conditioning?) Start by asking yourself *why* you are stressed. Is it because of lack of control? Is it because you are having difficulty coping with a certain situation or event? Is it because you don't feel you have the tools to deal what's going on in your life day to day? Is it because of a specific event or circumstance that is short term, or is it something specific that does not have a foreseeable end?

If you're stressed, it does not mean that you, as a person, are a stressful person. It simply means that there is a situation in your life that you don't have the means to handle at the moment. First of all, identify it, and identify why it's making you experience stress. Now ask yourself what you could do about that. Can you ask someone to assist you, is there some skill that would help, are you doing the wrong thing or reacting in a bad way? Do you have more control than you think you have? How could you try to get the situation under control, or get out of the situation totally if that's not possible?

Finally, how could you reframe it more helpfully? "I am stressed" is not very helpful to your state of mind, is it? Say that aloud and see how it makes you feel. How about "I am a little under pressure at the moment because…." Or "I have a difficult situation at the moment because…." and then complete your sentence with "but I am going to …… to improve the situation."

This can be applied even to the most difficult and fundamental issues in your life. What about someone who, when asked to define themselves, states "I am a drug addict".

Again, the first question that I would ask here is, why? Why do you take drugs? What are you trying to achieve? What do you need to get from the drugs – what is your underlying motivation? Some people say here that the motivation is the drugs themselves, but that's actually fairly unlikely, as you will understand by the time you reach the end of the next chapter.

My second question would be, is there anything that you could do instead? Is there anything else that could help, in place of the drugs? What would you need to have, to remove the need to take them?

My final point would be that you're not 'a drug addict', you're a person. Maybe a person who has a problem with drugs, but a person nevertheless. It is unfair and unhelpful to yourself to define yourself in terms of your problems. What about saying 'I am a person with a drug problem' or, better still, 'Currently, I have a problem with drugs, but I am working on that'.

Can you see the difference? I cringe when people describe themselves in terms of their failures or their problems. You are not an addict, or a failure, or a loser, or a waste of space. You are, no matter what, a person. Learn to recognize that feeling that comes over you when you define yourself as something really negative. This is a physical response by your body to something that your mind has said. Get accustomed to learning to pick up whenever this happens, and to instantly, consciously interrupt and challenge that thought.

If you show me someone who says they never have negative thoughts, either about themselves or someone else, I will show you someone in denial. We all have moments of fear, or doubt, or weakness. The trick is learning to stop them short the moment they arise, and making a more positive reaction.

If you keep thinking and responding in a certain way, eventually it will become automatic. One of the best things about this technique is that it becomes easier with repetition, until after a while you don't have to think about it at all.

What I really want you to understand is that you are not a slave to your personality. Yes, it's true that we have a core personality that underlies all of our identities and our roles, but even this is not fixed. If it is not working to your advantage, you have to change it. To do that, you need to acquire the ability to truly analyze it, and then work on the views that you have, the way that you see things, and the ways that you react. This will start to make the changes in you that you want to see.

You can make those changes in all three of the underlying areas, biological, thought processes and social conditioning. We will look at each of these individually in chapters 12 – 14. However, first I want to go through what I think it the most important thing in anyone's life, the underlying cause of all of your motivations, and the Holy Grail for those who want to completely transform their world. In the next chapter, we are going to look at state change.

The power in controlling your mind starts to become apparent when you begin to combine all of the information in the previous chapters and apply them in your life. Now that you have an understanding of beliefs, programming and identities, you can begin to look at how this affects your core personality, and to identify the things that are holding you back.

Earlier in the book, you wrote down your perspective on the traits that you have. If you have defined your personality in the past, it was most likely in light of your views on these traits. After reading this far, you will understand that these are actually beliefs that you have about yourself, and that some of them may be true, and some of them may be the result of past programming and self-stereotyping. All of them will be a combination of your genetics, your thought processes and your social conditioning. Once you know this, you can begin to look at your traits in a different light, and start to make the changes that you want.

Let's start by looking at this at a high level. Overall, do you like yourself as a person? Are you the sort of person that people want to be around? Do you inspire those around you, or do you make them feel bad about themselves? How do people see you?

Bear in mind that people can only go by what you put out into the world. If you're manifesting unhappiness, anger or impatience, this is what those around you will pick up on. If you think that you're really a nice person but people can't see that, then you're a victim of your own projections. Many of us are stressed and dissatisfied with life and take it out on those around us, all the time thinking that people should see the true character beneath the manifestations of negative emotion. Unfortunately, this isn't going to happen. Very few people in your life will know you well enough to see the 'real' you if that isn't what you're putting out there.

Would *you* like to be around you?

If you're reading this book, and you've got this far through it, the chances are that you want to make an improvement in your life and you're serious about making the changes that are needed. If this is so, bear in mind that our relationships with other people are an absolutely key part of the human experience, and that the quality of our relationships, whether they are in the home, at work, or social, materially alters our enjoyment of life, and how we get on in the world. I appreciate that it can be difficult if you have a roadblock in your life and are feeling resentful and frustrated, but you really do need to make the effort not to allow this to control your life. Taking things out on the people around you may be a natural human reaction, but it doesn't help you move forward, and it does not contribute to your happiness.

Remember also that you will have modeled what you saw as a child – or you may have anti-modeled it! If your mum or dad came home from work totally stressed and shouted at the children, you may have learned that this is the correct way to respond – or alternatively, you may have disliked being shouted at so much that you decided never to yell at your own children because you had a problem at work. Even in our modeling, we have a choice.

Statistics say that the majority of people who were beaten as children beat their own kids. This may be true, but there are many people who had a violent upbringing who reacted by becoming extremely anti-violence and would never hit their own family members, because they know what it feels like to have been on the receiving end; they would never inflict that unhappiness on their own family. You have a choice – and you go on having choices throughout life. If you have made wrong choices, there's no reason why you can't make a better one now. Your modeling shapes you, but it can only control you if you let it.

Modeling plays a great part in the extent to which we

are programmed as children, affecting our confidence, emotional responses and reactions. Think back now to your childhood, and the people that influenced you at that time.

Do you remember having a hero? If you thought very highly of someone – maybe a parent, aunt or uncle, older sibling or neighbor's child – there is a good chance that subconsciously you modeled their views, actions and opinions. Our thoughts are not all our own, as we cannot learn independently of our environment. If you have very deep-seated beliefs about something, can you remember a role model from whom you might have taken in these ideas? Conversely, if you are very against something, can you think of a person whose ideas or behavior you did not like?

The problem with this is that you can take on other people's opinions as to what makes you a success as a person. These are what have been called your 'conditions of worth'. If the conditions of worth that have been imposed on you are not in line with your own desires and values, this can cause immense amounts of problems in your life, as you struggle to be someone that you are not, in order to fulfill someone else's requirements.

One of the things that you need to be able to do is to assess your own dreams and ambitions, and make sure that they really are the things that you want. This is called 'congruence'. If you're incongruent, then you are fighting a losing battle because you don't really have motivation to achieve the things that you think you desire. You also may be trying to cultivate personality traits that you don't really want to have.

Imagine someone with a parent who owned an economically successful but ecologically unfriendly business. If that person at heart is a passionate environmentalist, but has taken on a goal of running and improving the business because their parent has made them believe this is the 'correct' dream, they will have a huge issue with incongruence. Modeling continues throughout life, and you may still be modeling people you should not be. Who have you modeled in the past? Who are you modeling now? Is what you are modeling congruent with what you really want?

We have various defense mechanisms which allow us to deal with things that we cannot cope with, and these work subconsciously. Therefore, you may not be aware of them. For example, we can transfer emotions that we feel about one person onto another person, if we find it easier to cope that way. You can be angry with your husband because you're angry with your dad, or your boss. You can transfer the passion that you feel for one thing into something else, because you feel the first thing is not right or possible. There are a number of different techniques that we subconsciously use, so for every dream and goal and emotion you have, ask yourself why it's important to you. Is this what you really want, or feel?

Understand yourself, understand your motivations, and learn to assess whether they truly are *your* motivations. Don't waste your energy on something that you don't really want.

The other thing to be aware of is that being too tough on yourself is not helpful to you. Many of us can be pretty hard on ourselves, and take the things that we do and achieve in life as a measure of our worth and our success as a person. Be very careful as to how you define yourself. There are many ways of looking at things, and quite often we choose negative ones. The way that we portray ourselves, that we tell our own story, is enormously important. Without changing a single actual thing in your life, you can change your whole outlook and perception. We do this by challenging our negative responses, and framing our perceptions into something more positive. Remember, perceptions are not the truth – they are filtered end products of our senses, cognitive processes and stored information.

If you're saying that there are some things that just don't have a positive side, you're right. Does that mean that you have to look at them in the worst possible light, and that you can't try to change your perspective? Absolutely not.

You might say 'I am stressed!' This could be read as, I am a stressful person. That's not actually correct. Stress is something that you are experiencing but it's not *you* (and even if you do this all the time, it's still not you, it's an unhelpful way that you have learned to react to a difficult situation – remember that conditioning?) Start by asking yourself *why* you are stressed. Is it because of lack of control? Is it because you are having difficulty coping with a certain situation or event? Is it because you don't feel you have the tools to deal what's going on in your life day to day? Is it because of a specific event or circumstance that is short term, or is it something specific that does not have a foreseeable end?

If you're stressed, it does not mean that you, as a person, are a stressful person. It simply means that there is a situation in your life that you don't have the means to handle at the moment. First of all, identify it, and identify why it's making you experience stress. Now ask yourself what you could do about that. Can you ask someone to assist you, is there some skill that would help, are you doing the wrong thing or reacting in a bad way? Do you have more control than you think you have? How could you try to get the situation under control, or get out of the situation totally if that's not possible?

Finally, how could you reframe it more helpfully? "I am stressed" is not very helpful to your state of mind, is it? Say that aloud and see how it makes you feel. How about "I am a little under pressure at the moment because…." Or "I have a difficult situation at the moment because…." and then complete your sentence with "but I am going to …… to improve the situation."

This can be applied even to the most difficult and

fundamental issues in your life. What about someone who, when asked to define themselves, states "I am a drug addict".

Again, the first question that I would ask here is, why? Why do you take drugs? What are you trying to achieve? What do you need to get from the drugs – what is your underlying motivation? Some people say here that the motivation is the drugs themselves, but that's actually fairly unlikely, as you will understand by the time you reach the end of the next chapter.

My second question would be, is there anything that you could do instead? Is there anything else that could help, in place of the drugs? What would you need to have, to remove the need to take them?

My final point would be that you're not 'a drug addict', you're a person. Maybe a person who has a problem with drugs, but a person nevertheless. It is unfair and unhelpful to yourself to define yourself in terms of your problems. What about saying 'I am a person with a drug problem' or, better still, 'Currently, I have a problem with drugs, but I am working on that'.

Can you see the difference? I cringe when people describe themselves in terms of their failures or their problems. You are not an addict, or a failure, or a loser, or a waste of space. You are, no matter what, a person. Learn to recognize that feeling that comes over you when you define yourself as something really negative. This is a physical response by your body to something that your mind has said. Get accustomed to learning to pick up whenever this happens, and to instantly, consciously interrupt and challenge that thought.

If you show me someone who says they never have negative thoughts, either about themselves or someone else, I will show you someone in denial. We all have moments of fear, or doubt, or weakness. The trick is learning to stop them short the moment they arise, and making a more positive reaction.

If you keep thinking and responding in a certain way, eventually it will become automatic. One of the best things about this technique is that it becomes easier with repetition, until after a while you don't have to think about it at all.

What I really want you to understand is that you are not a slave to your personality. Yes, it's true that we have a core personality that underlies all of our identities and our roles, but even this is not fixed. If it is not working to your advantage, you have to change it. To do that, you need to acquire the ability to truly analyze it, and then work on the views that you have, the way that you see things, and the ways that you react. This will start to make the changes in you that you want to see.

You can make those changes in all three of the underlying areas, biological, thought processes and social conditioning. We will look at each of these individually in chapters 12 – 14. However, first I want to go through what I think is the most important thing in anyone's life, the underlying cause of all of your motivations, and the Holy Grail for those who want to completely transform their world. In the next chapter, we are going to look at state change.

11 STATE CHANGE

A lot has been written about state change, whether or not it's called by that name in the book or article. Some of it is useful. Some of it, frankly, is fluff.

State change is, to my mind, the key to completely transforming your life, but it's not a magic wand. I have absolutely no doubt that learning to change your state, to give out more positive energy in order to attract more positive energy, will spectacularly improve your results and your whole life. If you understand it and use it correctly, it's a fantastic tool. The problem with state change is that a lot of unrealistic expectations can be set around the speed and scale of the results that you get from doing it. What happens then is that people suffer disappointment when things don't happen as they expected them to. And what do you think happens next? That's right, you form a belief about state change, that it doesn't work. And of course, we know that beliefs are a self-fulfilling prophecy.

It's my experience that many people feel a change almost immediately, a clear difference over a period of weeks or months, and a huge difference in the long term. However, if you learn how to change your state today, that does not mean that a Ferrari will fall out of the sky and land at your feet tomorrow. This is, I'm afraid, the wrong book if you are looking for an instant miracle cure to take, because no such thing exists. Some people are masters of state change and attracting the things they want into their lives, but it's a learned skill, and like all skills it takes dedication and practice. If you've never used state change before, if the Law of Attraction is completely new to you, and if your life at the moment is really awful, it's very unlikely that this will happen overnight. In the interests of scientific honesty, I have to tell you that if you win the lottery tomorrow, having done a state change exercise today, statistically it's much more likely to be a coincidence than a magical effect of reading this book. Although you can feel free to believe that if you want to and it will convince you of how powerful your mind is!

Much has also been written about affirmations, and again, some of it is misleading. I have spoken to people who firmly believe that if they say the same thing often enough, it will happen. Affirmations can be a good thing, but they have drawbacks. Firstly, they need to be in the present tense, which is fine unless they are something completely unimaginable to you now. If you have no food in the fridge and you're standing in the kitchen chanting "I am a multi-millionaire", your conscious mind will quite rightly say "No, you're not!" Secondly, many of the books don't explain affirmations correctly, leading people to believe that, if they just stay positive and keep repeating the affirmation, the thing will happen. Unfortunately, this is a misconception – affirmations do not make a physical thing happen.

The purpose of affirmations is to make a state change.

So, what is a state change? It is exactly what it says it is, a change in your state of mind. If you go from sad to happy, depressed to motivated, nervous to confident, that's a state change. They don't do very much to change the physical world. What they change is your mental state, which gives YOU the ability to make the physical changes.

Going back to that Ferrari, then, I'm afraid that saying "I have a Ferrari" twenty times morning and night, no matter how much feeling you put into it, is not going to make it materialize in the car park. A state change cannot change you from the owner of a rusty old Ford to the owner of a Ferrari. However, if you understand it, and do it correctly, it may turn you into the sort of person that could go out and attract the right sort of things and people into your life, and help you to build a career or a business that would fund your Ferrari purchase.

Having got any unrealistic expectations out of the way, I will now say that I believe state change to be the cornerstone of all successful transformations of people's lives. Thinking and feeling how you do now got you to exactly the place that you are today. If you want to be in a different place, you need to change the way that you think and the way that you feel. State change will do that.

You may not realize this, but much of what you do and what you want is for the purpose of achieving a state change. Actually, a desire for state change is the basis of most addictions. When you crave alcohol, drugs, chocolate, even excessive exercise, you are not usually craving the physical thing that you think you want. You are craving the state change.

Understanding this can be the key to realizing the things that drive us, and the things that are lacking in our lives. Most of what you want is to make you feel a certain way, although you may believe you want the thing itself.

This isn't just with regard to addictions. If you say you want money, why do you want the money? If you say because you want to buy a big house, why do you want the house? How would it make you feel to own the house? What does it symbolize to you? It may be proof of success, or perhaps something that you think will make other people respect you. We look for ways to experience the things that we want to feel, and we look for things to give that to us.

How else could you feel the way that you want to feel? If you are doing things to create a state change, and those things in themselves are not good for you, what could you replace them with? What else would give you what you want? If you could change your state without them, you would not need them. Be aware that your mind has the power to change your state itself, you only need external things because you are not aware of how to do this yet.

If there was a magic pill that you could take to make you happy, confident and successful, and this pill was both totally legal and totally free of adverse side effects, would you take it? I would say 99% of the people that I have asked this have answered that they would (and there will always be both cynics and people addicted to being miserable!). State change is not a magic pill, it requires consistent application and some effort on your part, but it will have that effect if you can master it.

Many of us are victims of our own minds. Never underestimate the power of the mind! If you don't train it correctly, it will master you, control you, and hold you back with all sorts of doubts and fears. If you are willing to put the time into reprogramming it, it will support you to get the things that you want out of life.

State change starts with a conscious decision to do something. You have looked at the causes of you believing as you do, assessed your own programming and stereotypes, identified your skills and the skills that you think you are lacking. You have all the information you need to make a state change.

Think back to Chapter 8. State change involves changing two things – your beliefs and your feelings. If you can change these, you will automatically change your attitudes, which will in turn change your behaviors and the results that you get from them. Changing your beliefs involves changing your thought processes, and we will look at specific techniques for doing this in Chapter 13. Changing your feelings is a complex interaction between your brain and your thought processes, and this will be covered in both Chapter 12 and Chapter 13. For now, let's look at what you are actually trying to achieve.

We have discussed reframing, and this is the essence of what you are learning to do, from the viewpoint of your mental processes. Most of the things that happen in your life can be looked at in a variety of ways. Some can be looked at as good or bad, either a difficulty or an opportunity, for instance, finding out that you are going to be made redundant from a job that you dislike. Some things are obviously bad, but even then, you have control over your reaction to them. All of us will have an instant, automatic reaction which is generated by the subconscious to any bad news. These reactions will vary between people, depending on their conditioning and biology.

Some of us always look for the negative in anything – even when we get good news, we immediately look for the potential negatives in it! (By the way, this is how I used to react, so even if you think you are the world's worst pessimist, I hope this will let you believe that you can change that!) Some of us are positive even in the face of all evidence that something bad is happening, and that is not helpful either (these are the people who would still have been sitting in their beds when the Titanic sank, confident that no little iceberg could sink their unsinkable ship).

You need to learn to change your reactions to those things that will be of most benefit to you. Note that there is no 'correct' reaction. There are just helpful reactions and unhelpful reactions.

You also need to change your beliefs, from unhelpful to helpful. Like reactions to situations, reactions to yourself and judgments on yourself are down to your own viewpoint. There are numerous ways that you can interpret your own characteristics and behavior, and numerous judgments that you can make on this basis.

The psychology of the mind works 'down the tree' – so if you look back to the diagram in Chapter 8, you will see that the actual work you need to do with your mind starts at the top, with the biology, thought processes and social conditioning. This will then filter down into your beliefs and your feelings. This is why we need to understand what our beliefs are, and what our feelings are. We also need to understand that these are open to a measure of control, beyond the instinctive reaction to them. The conscious decision is the way to challenge these ideas and break the cycle of programmed reaction.

Most of us would act angrily towards a man who hits his wife, and condemn him as a bad person. In many cases, the man will condemn himself as a bad person, too. He may not understand, when calm, why he reacts in this way, and be truly remorseful, only to repeat this behavior on the next occasion that he loses his temper. In reality, he may be seriously unhappy, stressed, suffering from psychological problems which he is unable to deal with, or have difficulty in expressing himself and his emotions. Violence can express frustration. It may be that he really wants to make a change, but cannot see how to do so. His current belief may be "I am violent, and therefore a bad person."

How might this man go about making a change? For a start, he could join a gym, which would give him a new outlet for his anger or frustration. Hard physical exercise is a great reducer of stress and actually makes a chemical change in your brain which can improve mood (more on this later!) This will allow him to be in a state where he is more able to look at the underlying causes of his aggression, and try to find better ways of dealing with them. The gym membership gives him that better way of dealing with frustration, and additionally gives him more control over his life and his reactions – plus it has the added benefit of stopping the police kicking down his door!

How about if you are a natural worrier? Some of us worry about things that haven't even happened yet and may not do so, it seems to be our natural state! If you are constantly in a state of nervous tension and expecting the worst to happen, be aware that this reaction is again a result of your programming and your genetics. In each situation, ask yourself, what are you actually worried about? Do you think that you are going to make a mess of things, that you won't be able to cope, that you are not in control? Why do you think the thing will happen anyway? The conscious decision here would be to make an intervention along the lines of "I will cope, I can do this, I will be able to deal with it if it does happen." Then work out the things that you could do. Write them down. Get advice, if necessary. This gives you a measure of control.

How do you react when people are unkind or unjust to you? How do you react when a problem arises? How do you cope when you're challenged? If you're not having helpful reactions, you need to learn to make the necessary interventions to get you a better result. You will learn how to do this, and how to challenge both your automatic physical and automatic mental responses. Be aware that once you understand how you react to things, you can start to *choose* a response, and that once you have done this a few times, that new response will become automatic – just like your old response was automatic.

If you think about it, there's no reason that this should not be the case. Your old reaction was programmed. Your new one will also become programmed – you are programming it by doing it. You can program your mind to intervene when you experience something, and to give a conscious instruction that will modify your unconscious reactions and emotional responses.

One of the interventions that I have learned is – "I can do this!" Short and effective. My programmed response to a problem (which would at one time have been to immediately stress about how I would deal with it) is to say this, and to stand up straight and feel confident. This gives a reaction on both the biological and psychological systems, which in turn has a knock-on effect on my social system, because I can handle more stress – and am therefore less limited in the situations that I can deal with. Once I've done that, I'm in a better place to logically consider the problem, and the options I have to deal with it.

Be aware also that things are not necessarily how they appear. Even things which may appear bad can have a positive effect in the future which it is impossible to grasp at the time.

For example, as I mentioned in an earlier chapter, when

a family member did something really awful to me, I reacted badly. I did not understand then how the mind works. I felt betrayed. My mood changed from anger to depression and back again. I actually became physically ill. The worst thing for me was trying to understand what I could possibly have done to make that happen. If I could have identified it, I would have actually felt better.

The problem was, I could not think of a single bad thing that I had ever done to that person. Humans try to justify things, both their own reactions and those of other people. After all, if you understand why it happened, you can make sure it does not happen again. It was the total lack of justification that I really could not cope with.

If it happened now, I would understand that we cannot always control the things that people do to us, but we can control our reactions to them. There is absolutely no way that any person could have such a devastating effect on me again. These days, I understand that we are not responsible for the reactions of other people, it does not reflect on us at all that they chose to behave in that way.

If people have treated you badly, it does not mean that you deserve it, and you do not have to find a reason for their actions. Sometimes you just need to accept that people can do awful things, and draw a line under it. Trying to understand their motivations is pointless, and a waste of your energy.

Now, I actually use that awful time as a positive. It's a benchmark of what I can handle. When things are difficult in my life (as they are for all of us from time to time) I think back to those days and realize that my current situation does not touch that experience for trauma. Given that I handled it and got through it, I know I can handle whatever it is that I am going through now – in fact, when I compare the situations, the current problem usually seems trivial. There's a rather nice irony in the fact that we are able to use bad experiences in the past as positive proof that we are able to deal with unpleasant situations.

If you look back on all the difficult things that you have gone through in your life, you maybe take these as reasons to think that life is difficult. Can you instead take them as proof that you are resilient, and that you can take what the world throws at you? You're here, and you're reading a book designed to help you take your life where you want it to go. I'd say that means you are both a person who is capable of taking positive action, and a survivor.

Certain schools of psychology state that it is not the actual things that happen to us in life that cause us to have issues with them – rather, it is the meanings that we give to those events. In my experience, this is absolutely accurate. If you remove the meaning from the event, you remove the emotional response. You will not always be consciously aware of what you have interpreted the meaning as being, but regardless of this, it will be the source of your emotion around the event. Negative meanings produce a negative emotional response. Therefore, it is absolutely essential that you learn to change the meaning.

In the event mentioned above, the meaning I initially ascribed to it was that this was a personal attack on me, which I must unknowingly have done something to cause. The meaning that I ascribe now is that the person in question is angry and bitter about life in general, and that this does not reflect on me in any way. I have removed the negative meaning, and therefore the negative emotion. This changes my feelings of anger and hurt into feelings of pity that someone could feel so bad about their own life that it would cause them to try to ruin someone else's.

Depression is considered to be caused either by lack of positive reinforcement, or by non-contingent punishment. That is, either we were not given the necessary support to let us know that we should be confident in ourselves and our abilities, or we were made to feel that whatever we did, something bad would happen to us anyway. This leads to a state of mind known as learned helplessness. You don't feel that you have any control over your own life, and the direction that it will go in. Again, I have found that many people do indeed feel this way, and the whole purpose of this book is to teach you methods to take that control back, and to be in charge of your emotions, your reactions, and your future.

There is one psychological approach which states that suffering is part of life, and that problems come because people fight against that. Anxiety is considered to stem from striving to get things that you don't have, rather than just accepting life as it is. Certainly, I would agree that there are always going to be problems, and that you have to accept that. However, I don't agree that trying to change your life if it isn't going the way you want is the cause of suffering.

To me, the biggest problem that people have is that the change is beyond their control or their capability. Would you still be stressed if you knew how to make the change? In most cases, I have found the answer to be No. I would add the caveat though that stressing over not having the things you want immediately, and putting yourself under enormous pressure to get them straight away, is not healthy. You need to enjoy the journey as much as arriving at the destination. If you find every step difficult, you're on the wrong path.

You will notice one word appearing consistently through this chapter, and that is Control. This, to me, is the key to state change. You have to feel in control. I would go so far as to say that there are two things in my opinion which cause psychological distress – lack of control, and lack of hope. If you can see a way out of something, it is not anywhere near as frightening as if you feel trapped in a bad situation, with no control to change it and no hope that things will ever be different.

Anxiety and depression are considered to be forms of mental illness, but given that everyone is worried or unhappy at some time in their lives, how do we denote the difference between those states, and simple human emotional responses to things that happen in our lives? Why do we refer to it as an illness? The key is control. Anxiety and depression are simply worry and unhappiness that have got out of control to the point where they impact our lives.

Learn to stay calm, and to look for the solution, rather than focusing on the problem. Plan to be in control. Planning solutions will give you a feeling of control, and it will also give you hope. Find new ways to view your present experience.

So, what can you do if you feel you have no control? Taking control of yourself is the first step. This includes being accountable for yourself and for your own results. Over the next three chapters, we will look at how to approach this from the biological, psychological and social angles.

12 BIOLOGY

Every human being has an underlying genetic make-up. These days, most people have heard the terms DNA and heredity. To try to understand who we are, and why, and how far we are defined by the genetic material we inherit from our parents, it's helpful to understand a little more about how this biological system works.

Despite our differences, the basic make-up of a person is the same. The genetic material that defines us, DNA, is contained within the nucleus of the cells that make up our bodies. DNA is basically a coding instruction. Molecules of DNA are clustered into genes, and genes are compiled into linear strings called chromosomes. Humans have 46 chromosomes – 22 pairs of identical chromosomes, plus two chromosomes which define gender.

For every trait that you inherit, there is a gene. We inherit two genes for each trait, one from each parent. Your parents will also have had a pair of each gene, and passed only one of these down to you. Each gene contains a set of instructions for coding. This is your genotype – the inheritable information that you were given and which will control how you are 'coded', and which you will pass on to your own children. The results of that – your appearance, traits and behavior - are your phenotype. Basically, the genotype codes for the phenotype. So, your cells are built according to the instructions in your genes, dictated by genotype, to produce your phenotype. Your phenotype is also influenced by the surrounding environment.

The cell type that we are interested in, in order to understand the effect of our inherited biology on our lives, is called the neuron. Neurons are the main cell in your central nervous system – they are found mostly in the brain but also in the spinal cord. Neurons have a very specific function – they transmit information through the body. If someone dropped a drawing pin on the carpet, and then you stood on it, it was neurons that sent the message to the relevant muscles to tell them to pull your foot back, and neurons that relayed the message back to your brain that your foot was hurting. Neurons take in information from your senses, code it, and store it. Neurons register that you are hungry, thirsty or tired, and prompt you to do something about it. Neurons are at the base of all your reactions.

Neurons are also responsible for releasing chemical substances called neurotransmitters. Neurons form connections throughout your brain, and neurotransmitters serve the purpose of telling the next neuron in line to activate, or not to activate. Different neurotransmitters have different functions, and also have different effects in different areas of the brain, but the variation of levels of these neurotransmitters has an impact on how you feel. For example, one cause of depression has been stated to be reduced levels of the neurotransmitter serotonin in certain parts of the brain - hence many anti-depressant drugs work in such a way as to block serotonin being reabsorbed after release, which increases serotonin levels in the brain with the purpose of reducing depression.

Neurotransmitters pass across a space between neurons called synapses. Synapses are important both in that they form the area where neurotransmitter levels are held, and because they are the thing that makes connections between neurons, allowing information to pass through your brain, triggered by the passing of the neurotransmitter across the synapse to activate or deactivate the neuron or neurons on the other side. These are known as synaptic connections.

The main difference between neurons and many of the other cells in your body is that they are not designed to be replaced if they die. However, biological psychologists have found a very interesting phenomenon. Neurons are not limited to the neural connections they formed while you were growing up. They are capable of making new ones. If certain cells die, neurons can make alternate pathways through the brain to compensate. Even if that doesn't mean that you can get all of the full functioning of your brain back, say after an accident or illness that causes physical damage to it, it means that your brain can to some degree compensate. This is known as brain plasticity.

This is not intended to be a book about human biology, and we don't need to consider any of the above in any more detail. However, there are certain important points that you can take from the biological background.

- Genes influence our physical make-up, which in turn influences behavior.
- Neurotransmitter levels, which affect the way that we feel at certain times, are not fixed, they change all the time.
- Brain connections are not fixed, the brain is capable of making new ones.

This will, I hope, allow you to understand that you are not totally the product of your genetics. You have the ability to make changes in your life which will actually impact, not only your experience, but also something physical – the brain connections that you have, and the levels of certain neurotransmitters in your brain that control your moods.

Carrying on a certain behavior again and again has made actual physical changes in your brain. The good news here is, of course, that these are not fixed. If you begin to perform different actions, again and again, you will find that the effect of previous actions can be reversed.

Think about someone coming back to education after a long period of time. Initially, learning may seem difficult. However, if you stick at it, you will find that the process becomes easier. Your brain will begin to use pathways for processing and storing information that have maybe been fairly inactive since school. As your brain adapts, learning becomes easier. This is because exercising your brain has an actual physical effect. It is believed that learning and memory formation actually changes the pattern of connections between neurons.

This is like any form of exercise. The more you practice, the better you get. So, if you think that you are not capable of going out and learning the things that you need to know, in order to achieve the things you want, think again. The only way you are going to know is by giving it a try. If you give your brain the chance, it may just surprise you.

Unfortunately, we are not always in control of the effects on our brain. You need only look at Post Traumatic Stress Disorder to understand that traumatic experiences have consequences for the nervous system. Changes in synapses actually alter the way that we view the world.

The good news is that if negative events and experiences can change the nervous system, so can positive ones. Here you see the connection between biology and social environment – outside events impact inside events. Inside events in turn have an impact on outside events – brain conditioning by learning, as mentioned above, changes the outside (social) world in that you are able to make a change in your life because your brain is learning the things that you need to learn. If you add in that the way you think, and the way that you train yourself to react to events, will influence your responses and the instructions that you give to your brain, you will begin to understand how biopsychosocial influence works, and why it is so important to look at all three aspects.

Firstly, you need to be aware of your psychological state, because that will have physical effects on your system. Some of these you may be aware of, some you will not. For instance, the levels of the hormone testosterone have been shown in experiments to actually change as the result of winning or losing in a competition. The winner may experience a sense of excitement and achievement, the loser a sense of sadness or embarrassment, and put the physical feeling down purely to the psychological experience of winning or losing. It's not. You are actually making a physical change in your body as a result of your emotions.

Something else that you need to be aware of is the fact that some behaviors which are underpinned by evolution can actually be bad for us now. Evolution is a great thing, but it's very slow to change – so rather than being programmed for the modern world, your biology is set for a hunter-gatherer society. This does not involve computers, sitting in offices all day, or polite social behaviors. Eating as much fatty food as possible so that you don't starve to death over the winter will just make you fat if you spend five days a week sitting at a desk, and the weekend sitting in front of the TV. Hostility, fear, aggression, which at one time would have led to a fight or flight response, can no longer be solved by running away or hitting the other guy over the head. Your body still automatically carries out all of the functions designed to allow fight or flight – releasing huge amounts of adrenalin, speeding your heart rate, improving blood flow to the muscles – but you (hopefully) don't need to run or fight. Instead, you complain to your friends and colleagues, or call your solicitor – and you leave fatty substances sitting around in your blood stream that will increase the risk of a heart attack.

The other problem with our evolutionary progress being out of date is that, left to ourselves, we can exhibit a lot of behaviors that are underpinned by evolution, which in modern society are out of place. Jealousy, rage, depression and feelings of rejection can be the result. If you don't control your biology, it will control you. Fortunately, we have the ability as humans to carry out interventions, by way of our reasoning processes, that allow us to make better choices and more sensible reactions. That is, we do IF we learn how we naturally respond to circumstances and change the reactions that we don't like.

A lot of negative emotions have physical effects on the body. For instance, when you become angry, you may get hot, feel your heart speeding up and your breathing get faster. You may even start to shake. If you are alert to these physical responses, you can learn to react to them in such a way as to break this automatic response and get yourself back under control.

However, some responses are not so easy to feel. If you are constantly under stress, you may not notice your body's reactions so much. In fact, some people actually like being under stress, as it makes them feel motivated and energized. Be aware that there is a big different between healthy pressure, which can actually improve your performance, and unhealthy stress. Stress is still giving you all the effects of these fight or flight responses, and over a period of time that's going to cause physical damage to your body. The stress hormone, cortisol, was not designed to be constantly released, but sometimes in highly stressed people the usual relaxation effect which switches off cortisol production does not occur. This leads to high blood pressure, impaired cognitive (thought process) functioning, and suppressed thyroid function, which can cause weight gain.

Short periods of stress, say to get a project finished on time, are one thing. Living your life constantly on the edge is something else altogether. If you are an adrenalin junkie, take a step back and think what you are doing to your body. It's not designed to live life on constant high alert.

The other factor to take into account here is your neurotransmitters. You may not be aware of them, but you are very aware of their levels, due to how you are feeling at the time. We mentioned earlier that reduced levels of serotonin are associated with depression, and that increasing serotonin levels is the function of many anti-depressant drugs. You might be interested to know that chocolate also increases serotonin levels. So, the next time you are stressed at work and head for the vending machine, it might not be because you are hungry. 'Chocolate makes me feel better' is not just an excuse for eating unhealthily. It actually does have a physical effect. The downside, of course, is that if you do this too often, it can have the additional physical effect of making you overweight.

Dopamine is a neurotransmitter that has an effect on pleasure and reward effects. It is a very useful chemical in that it influences motivation, helping you to work towards your goals, regardless of what they are. Incidentally, the drugs cocaine and amphetamine both increase dopamine levels in the brain (so does caffeine, to a much lesser degree), hence the feeling of euphoria reported by those who use them. Doing things that you enjoy can increase dopamine levels without the need to resort to artificial stimulants. It is important to make sure that you set time aside for family, friends and enjoyable activities, rather than just working. Serotonin production is also stimulated by doing things that we like.

People suffering from depression are often recommended to take exercise. This is because exercise naturally stimulates the production of endorphins and also reduces levels of cortisol, the stress hormone (it also increases dopamine and serotonin levels). Endorphins' main function is as the body's natural painkiller, but additionally it helps to create a general feeling of well-being. The best type of exercise for raising endorphin levels is aerobic, but any type of exercise is better than none. Make sure that you set aside at least ten minutes every day for some type of exercise – thirty is better, but even ten will make a difference. If you're feeling unhappy, or tired, or confused, try going out for a brisk walk. You will find that your body starts to relax as your cortisol levels drop, and that your depressed feelings start to lift as your endorphin levels rise. If you think that you don't have time for exercise, make it. You will find that the increase in productivity caused by being able to think more clearly and without stress hampering your responses more than makes up for the time out that you took.

So, where do you actually start to make changes to your physical responses? Take a moment now to think how you actually feel at this given moment. Optimistic about being able to make some changes? Worried about your ability to do something? Stressed over a decision? Confident about your future and your own talents? Happy because you have a lovely family or good friends? Excited? Apprehensive? Maybe a little of all of these things?

Now, sit up straight, or stand. Take a deep breath. Feel yourself relax. Stretch up your shoulders and roll them a little to remove tension. Stretch your arms up, then relax them. Take another deep breath.

Now, smile. Think about something that makes you happy. Feel the changes in your body as you do so. You should be able to feel even more of the stress and tension leave you. Think about something that you find amusing and laugh out loud. If there's a mirror handy, go and look into it and smile at yourself. Say something nice to yourself, or something reassuring like "We can do this!" Smile again. Now assess again how you feel, right at this moment.

Congratulations, you have just changed your neurotransmitter levels. You didn't take any drugs, legal or illegal. You didn't need to eat chocolate, or even exercise. You changed your physiological state, and that caused a biological reaction. I have seen very few people who do not feel a positive change after this exercise.

Of course, your neurotransmitter levels will drop again,

but now you know how easy it is to change them, you can do it again. You can also start to become alert to the physical state of your mood, which will help you to intervene quickly to change it.

Think about when someone says or does something to you that you do not like. I feel that physically, and I know a lot of other people do too. Think back to the positive changes that you made in the exercise that we just did. The changes caused by experiencing something unpleasant are just the opposite. Cortisol levels increase, and levels of dopamine, serotonin and endorphins drop. You may feel a fluttery chest, a sense of anxiety, irregular breathing, and other unpleasant sensations.

As soon as this happens, I pick up on it and I interrupt it. This is just practice, and there is no reason that you cannot do this too. Mentally take a step back, and CHOOSE how to react. Frankly, if people say unpleasant things now, it doesn't have too much effect. If it's something that I think is unfair or untrue, I reject it. If I think it's true, I acknowledge that, accept it and change it.

If I have a problem, I work out all the options that I have got to fix it. If it's sad news, I accept it, and deal with it. This is the effect of consciously intervening in your reactions and changing them. You do not have to be a slave to your physical mind. It will work for, rather than against you, if you let it, but you have to take charge of it. Your reactions are automatic, and your brain will just do what it's been programmed to do to date, if you let it.

Do you remember that in the last chapter I asked what you would do if you had a magic pill that you could take to make you feel better? Without using drugs, legal or illegal, this is the closest that you are going to get to it. Once you understand that your own reactions can have the same effect on your body as illegal drugs or prescription medication, without any risk of addiction or harmful side-effects, aren't you going to use it as much as you can?

Personally, I think it's pretty amazing that we can make

such big changes with so little effort. Human biology is a powerful thing. If you have followed the exercise above, you will have seen for yourself that changing your biology can change your mood.

If you have thought till now that you were a victim of your own genetics, you now know that this is not true. You are influenced by them, but can in turn influence them and bring about change. Knowing this, make sure you start every day in the most positive way that you can. When you get out of bed, stand up straight, smile, and think positively. After you clean your teeth in the morning, look in the mirror and let yourself know that you can do the things that you are setting out to do. Learn to notice during the day when you are feeling stressed or unhappy, and take five minutes to yourself to repeat this exercise. Make sure you go to sleep on a happy thought or resolution.

Make sure that your biology is working for you, and not against you.

13 COGNITION

Cognitions are the mental processes which dictate how we process information – what we perceive, what we remember, what we say, how we react. These develop as we grow, based on what we experience, our biology and our social conditioning.

What you are today is a product of what you were born with and the things that have happened to you during your life, shaping your reactions, your emotional response to events and the way that you think. If you actively engage with your cognitive processes, you have the ability to gain a greater degree of control. In fact, the key to being able to get the things that you want, if you have not been able to do so to date, is to change the way that you think about them, and about yourself.

If you look at people who have overcome huge obstacles in their lives, and gained things that you would like to achieve, you may think that this means that they are fundamentally different from you – luckier, more gifted, more brave. The chances are that in reality they just have more supportive thought processes. Where you might be worrying about things going wrong, or doubting your own ability, they will be making a conscious decision that nothing is going to stop them, that they have the ability to achieve their goal, and that they will acquire the skills, information and contacts that they need to do so.

When I say "it's all in your mind", I want you to understand that changing your thought patterns from fear, doubt and lack of self-confidence to motivation, determination and confidence can have the most enormous impact on your life. If you never take any action, you will never get any rewards. If you don't think that the action would have a positive ending, you won't take it. Often the assumption that the action would not end well is based purely on self-belief, informed by past experience, our biology and our social experience.

Most of us, somewhere inside, have a fear of failure. It's likely that the successful person you have set up as a role model was not absolutely certain, when he or she set out to do the thing that you admire, that it would be a success. If you think that being nervous about something means that you are not cut out to achieve what you want you want from life, think again. Those who are blindly optimistic and don't ever consider the options if something goes wrong are most likely to have a spectacular disaster at some point in their lives.

Yes, you can be lucky. However, never to think about the risks of what you are doing, and how you can mitigate against things going wrong, is to leave yourself without an escape route if you need it. Being afraid is not a barrier to success so long as you can move past this, set the right mindset, and acquire the knowledge that you need to mitigate against the risks involved.

We're not born with that fear of failing – babies don't not try to stand, or to talk, in case they can't do it. We're also not born with a sense of embarrassment when we do fail – you would not expect that same baby to blush and hide his face every time he fell over or got a word wrong. We learn our fears of failure, losing and making ourselves look ridiculous as we grow up. These are social conditioning fears, learned from those around us, and they translate into the mental processes which are programmed to tell us not to try in case we end up failing or looking stupid.

Humans have found ways to deal with their disappointments and with the lack of satisfaction in their lives. We tell ourselves that we don't really want that thing, or that it wouldn't be what we hoped for if we had it. We transfer our energies into something else that we think we *can* get. We blame outside circumstances – our families, lack of education, lack of sufficient intelligence, the boss, the business partner, the financial adviser, the government, the economic climate, fate. These are all defense mechanisms to protect us from the unpleasant thought that we don't have what we want, and we can't see how to get it.

Defense mechanisms are not totally a bad thing – they are a consolation when we feel disappointed about ourselves and our achievements. They help us to cope. However, they are not necessarily a helpful thing. If you constantly give yourself excuses about why you can't do things, you remove all of the options to sit down and plan how you *could* do them.

The problem with defense mechanisms is that many of them are unconscious. We spend so long telling ourselves that we can't reach a certain goal or have a certain thing that we begin to believe that, and therefore don't even look around us for opportunities. Do you remember that we discussed attention and perception? If you don't think you are capable of taking up opportunities, you won't pay attention to them, and therefore you won't even see them. They will be filtered out as though they
were not even there. How many people do you know who are currently complaining that there are no opportunities in the current climate, while those with different thought processes are getting on with doing well for themselves?

If you think that you could not be suppressing all of this frustration inside you without knowing about it, think again. One of the most extreme defense mechanisms is repressive coping, where people actually suppress strong emotions that they are having difficulty dealing with. This is rather frequent among people who have had a troubled childhood, and continues into later life. These people genuinely believe they are not suffering under the effects of that negative emotion – but frequently begin to exhibit the physical symptoms associated with anxiety.

Suppressing desires, hopes and dreams is not good for you. Your body and your mind are closely connected, and there is much evidence to support the fact that many bodily illnesses can stem from mental frustrations, even those that you may not be aware of.

You might be asking at this point, how can I possibly know what is stored inside my head, if it's unconscious? Look at your results. Look at your natural reaction to things. Do you feel as if things are going well for you? Do you respond with an open mind to new situations and events, or do you instantly look for the negative? Feeling generally dissatisfied with the things that you are achieving, or always being pessimistic, are signs that your subconscious processes are probably not where you want them to be. If that is the case, then you need to start some re-programming and re-stereotyping.

There is only one way that you can change your subconscious mind, and that's with your conscious thoughts. Focus on your conscious awareness. Start to pick up on the things that are causing the issues in your life. If you think back to the last chapter, we spoke about how you can actually feel physical signs in your body when your mind is disturbed or made unhappy by something. You are your own radar. Start to become sensitive to how you are feeling. If you detect yourself feeling unhappy or uncomfortable, what were you thinking about at the time? How did it make you feel, and why?

You may think that you are always in full control of your conscious awareness, but this is very unlikely. Our levels of conscious awareness change all the time – sometimes we are very aware of how we are feeling inside and what we are experiencing outside, and sometimes we are not at all aware. Various external influences can change our conscious state – things as diverse as experiencing a tragedy or being drunk. Also, think about the times when you go off in a daydream, maybe sitting at your desk, or in a chair at home, and you suddenly come out of it to find that minutes have passed without you realizing it. Were you aware of your bodily feelings or of what was going on around you during that time?

The key area to understand in cognition is that, because our conscious state changes all the time, all by itself, in response to external influence, you need to BECOME that influence. If you master your conscious thoughts, your subconscious thoughts will by themselves change over time. You are stereotyping and programming, in exactly the same way that you were programmed and stereotyped to create the subconscious states that you have now. The difference is that you are stereotyping and programming what you want, rather than what other people want you to have, or offload onto you.

The first place to start is with your thoughts and your words. Your conscious state will be programmed by how you think and speak about it, so learn to be very careful of what you think and what you say!

If you constantly think, for whatever reason, that you are a failure, incompetent, not very gifted, what are you programming yourself with? How are you stereotyping yourself?

If someone that you trusted kept telling you that Max in the office wasn't very talented and that he shouldn't be relied on to get anything right, what assumptions would you make about Max? Would you be hesitant about trusting him to do some important work for you? Most people would, if the information came from someone that they considered to be a reliable source. The problem here is that your subconscious thinks that your conscious is a reliable source. If you constantly tell it that you're really not very good, it will believe you, and it will respond accordingly to every situation.

Of course, it may be other people telling you that you are not capable of doing the things that you want to do. Sometimes you don't even have to trust them – some people habitually listen to the opinions of others, without even considering whether they are qualified to have an opinion, or what their motives might be.

The answer to all of these things is simple. Take

charge of your conscious thoughts! If you don't, they will absolutely, without a doubt, take charge of you.

Remember, what you are really trying to achieve is a state change, and the most finely tuned tools that you have for doing that, for achieving something specific, are your conscious thoughts, and your words.

Think about the number of times that you think "It's not worth trying" or "I could never do that". If you tell yourself that enough, you'll believe it. Learn to challenge yourself. Replace "I couldn't…" with "How could I…?" – or better still with "I will!" You have plenty of time to work out the How later. For now, just worry about the decision – and once you have made it, keeping making it! Every time that self-doubt or indecision creeps in, detect it and stamp on it. "I can" and "I will" can drown out an awful lot of negative chatter coming from your subconscious, and will turn the focus onto how what you want can be achieved.

It's also very important to be aware of your language. Spend some time listening to the people around you, and you will see what I mean. Some people are really confident, and speak about themselves very positively. Even when they have had something go wrong, they are sure that they will come out on the other side of it. I don't mean people who brag – I'm sure we all know a few of those! – but those who genuinely have a quiet, calm self-belief.

Now listen for someone who puts themselves down all the time. You will hear a lot of words like "I can't" or "I wish" or "If only". This is not a good way to speak! Try to never tell yourself that you can't do something, or remind yourself of the things that you have not achieved. Language is a very precise tool, different ways of phrasing things – even if you only change one word – can have a huge impact on what you are telling your subconscious.

Also, don't constantly put yourself down. There is a big difference between being modest and constantly speaking about your lack of accomplishments or abilities. Try to never speak badly about yourself. Just because you have not done something yet, does not mean that you never will. Just because you don't know how to do something doesn't mean you can't learn.

Think about how you would speak about a much-loved friend, failures and faults and all. That's how you should speak about yourself. If you don't love yourself, how can other people love you? If you see only the things that you don't like, how can others see the things that are likeable? Emphasizing the bad things does you no favors – not in how you think, how you react, how you feel inside, or how others see you. Speech is the great evolutionary advantage of the human race. Language is a gift. Use it correctly.

You should also remember that nothing is 'real'. You will construct your own meaning for everything that happens to you. If you're one of those people who always sees the worst in situations, try asking yourself how else you could see them.

Think now about something that's happened that you felt was a bad thing. How else could you think about it? Maybe something good came from it – even if it was only to make you tougher! How about the situation that you find yourself in now? How are you looking at it? How might someone else construct it? Remember that that is what it is – it's *your* construction, your view and interpretation, of how the situation is at the moment. That does not mean that it's the only way it can be constructed, or that you don't have the power to construct it differently.

Of course, it is necessary to be realistic. There are certain things that we cannot change right now, and certain things that we cannot change at all. If you are a six foot four lady, you are probably never going to become the female lead in the Bolshoi Ballet. If you are currently unemployed and living in a rented flat, chances are that you're not going to have a mansion and a boat tomorrow (although that doesn't mean that you can't have those things - it just means that if you expect them tomorrow you are setting yourself up for a huge disappointment when you wake up in the morning!) Aspiring to be the lead scientist at NASA is probably not the best career plan if you failed basic physics.

Accept that there are things that you cannot change, and things that won't change in a moment, and things that it's not sensible to want to change. Disappointment will not help most people get to where they want to be, although it can be used as an incentive.

Sometimes, the motivation to get out of a situation or to avoid a failure is bigger than the motivation to stay safe. However, you need to accept that we are all born with certain physical traits that we cannot change, certain disadvantages that can take time to overcome, and certain areas which we will find difficult, as well as ones for which we have a natural aptitude. It would be a very boring world if we were all the same, and if we were all good at everything! Yes, you can do things that you don't like and get on in life, but surely it's better to do things that you enjoy? You can push yourself too hard, and maybe get what you want with a worn-out body and mind. Or you can enjoy what you do and have fun on the journey as well as when you reach the end of it. Dream big, but make sure you dream to your advantage (and as said earlier, make sure it's YOUR dream!)

You also need to take responsibility for your own decisions, actions and results. It might feel better initially if you blame something else, but to totally deny responsibility actually takes power from you. In order to have the power to do the things that you want to do, you need to realize that YOU are the sole person responsible for your destiny. Other people and outside events can influence it, but you are in charge. They are the road, you are the driver. Only you get to say where you are going, and only you get to decide how to get there. Some of us get into the habit of blaming external events or people, and this may be a comfort, but it's also not good for you. The more control you assign to things outside of yourself, the less power you have for yourself. If you can put less effort into worrying whose fault it was, and more effort into taking control, you will see a huge change in your results.

You, and only you, have the power to change your conscious awareness, and to put yourself into the right mindset to achieve your goals.

All of your assumptions are based on your past experience and programming. If you let them, they will keep you on exactly the same path that you are on now. It takes a mental effort to stop, reassess, and make the changes.

Before reacting to a situation, take a breath. What do you recall about similar situations or encounters in the past, and how is that telling you to react? How is it making you feel? If you had done something differently, would you have got a different and more beneficial result? How would that have worked? Could you do that now?

One of the biggest problems for humans is that we get stuck in past events. We have the ability to analyze, endlessly stress over, and painfully regret, things that have happened and decisions that we made. Some of this is conscious, but it passes down to the subconscious and is stored as 'true' information. All of the times that you were hard on yourself, every negative reference you make, is coded into your subconscious – and the more times you repeat the process, the more ingrained the belief gets.

You need to change the meaning.

Remember our theory of emotion? It's not the event itself that causes the emotion, it's the meaning that you have attached to it. If you can change that meaning, say from a failure to a learning experience, you will change the emotion.

If you want to know how you really feel about something, visualize it. We make associations between images and feelings. Think hard about the thing that you want, picture it in your mind, and see what you feel as a result of doing that. If those feelings are negative – fear, or doubt, or uncertainty, or an inability to really be able to see and feel yourself doing that thing – why? Is the problem with lack of knowledge, lack of self-belief, or with negative associations?

You must be aware that you can get stuck in negative meanings and responses, and that if you do this, it will remove all of the control that you have over your own destiny. Ask yourself again, *why* do I believe that? Where have I learned it? How else could I look at it? These are not things that we are taught to ask ourselves.

When I was first starting out on my career, I stuck religiously to staff jobs. I got lots of promotions, and did what was considered to be very well. However, it annoyed me that I was doing so well and making so much money for other people, and also that I was tied to their hours, their office, their rules. It occurred to me that I might like to start out in business for myself.

The problem was, as soon as I got a certain way into planning for the business, I would always find a reason not to do it. The reasons varied – there wasn't enough demand, the market was saturated, the climate was not right – but the end result was always the same. I decided that going into business for myself was not a good idea.

When I got interested in psychology, I began to wonder why this was. For someone who had done a degree in business studies, it was a strange attitude to have. I had proved my capability in other people's businesses, successfully helped others with start-ups and growth, and had a whole lot of saleable knowledge, but I did not seem to want to make use of that for myself. One day, for the first time, I sat down and really *thought* about it – not about doing a specific business, but about how I felt about business, and why.

When I was young, my stepfather had a number of businesses which did really well for a time, and then failed.

We moved between having lots of money and being broke. Every time things sorted themselves out, my stepfather would start a new business, and the cycle would start again.

My mum at this time had stopped working due to ill-health, but previously she had always been in employment. She compared the benefit of getting a regular payment every month, which was always reliable, to the boom and bust of a business, and would have loved my stepfather to get a regular paid job. My stepfather, as the son of a very successful self-made businessman, found being an employee bad for his self-esteem and incongruent with his own wishes, whatever the benefits of regular pay.

So, what did I learn about employment and business?

Firstly, of course, I learned that business is risky. I associated being in business with never knowing how much money you would have coming in, periods of financial hardship, and arguments about money. I learned that being an employee is the only way to guarantee a secure income, even though you may hate your job and your boss, and never feel satisfied with what you are doing. That's a lovely combination of thoughts to have, isn't it? So, as a response, I plugged away at my career, doing really well, getting promotions, getting regular money, and hating every minute of working for someone else.

Within three months of realizing this, I was self-employed, and I have never been on anyone's payroll since. I taught myself a better way of thinking – that business is risky, but that the risk can be mitigated if you have all the knowledge and information that you need, and for me the benefits by far outweigh the risks. Not that there is anything wrong with being an employee – if I had been happy working for other people, I would probably still have been climbing the promotion ladder and doing well. But if you're not happy, then you are not getting as much out of life as you could. I have come to the conclusion that it doesn't really matter what you do, so long as you enjoy it, and it meets the level of income that you need. However, if you don't know both what you want, and why you want it, how can you expect to be happy with it? If that nagging feeling of dissatisfaction is following you about, ask yourself, why am I here, and where would I rather be?

You will notice that the word 'control' has again been appearing a lot in this chapter. If you want to be happy, you need to be in control of your life. If you are not challenging the programming that stops you doing what you want to do, you're not in control. The biggest cause of suicide is hopelessness. If you have control, you have hope. You need to learn to solve problems.

Remember that everyone has problems, mistakes and failures in their past – some have traumatic events that they find it hard to deal with. Now that you understand conditioning and stereotyping, you will have a better idea of the effect that these things might have had on your views of yourself and the things and people around you, and why they may have taken away your belief that you have control over your life. Now that you understand cognition, you can see how, if you let it, these events will control your life going forward. You can also see that you have the ability to step in, challenge them, and change the result. Find more positive beliefs, and more positive ways of looking at things.

Don't look at your mistakes as evidence of your lack of skill or your ability. Look at them as learning experiences. If you just dwell on your failures, you get no benefit from them – you are merely replaying a negative experience, and why would you want to put yourself through that? Asking yourself what you can learn from that experience will help to ensure that you don't repeat your mistakes. It will also make you feel a lot happier than if you just use them to hit yourself over the head.

I speak to a lot of people who have done things in life that they are ashamed of – maybe they treated someone very badly, or stole from a friend. Your behavior is not you – just because you acted badly does not mean you are a bad person – you are a person who did a bad thing. Also, if you were still the same person who did that thing, you probably would not feel bad about it. If you are subconsciously punishing yourself for a past action, stop. Hurting yourself won't do anything to improve things for the person that you injured. Go out there and do something positive for someone. If you want to be a better person, that's a much more productive way of doing it.

One of the hardest things I see is those people who have experienced a terrible event, or events, in the past. I see people who have endured awful suffering, trapped in a cycle of despair, depression or anger. You cannot change the past – it has happened and there is nothing that you can do about it. However, you can refuse to let it keep control of your present.

Whatever is still hurting you, try to let it go. Remove the emotional response from it, and understand that the world has bad things and bad people, but also wonderful things and people. Your life is in front of you, do not give the past the power to stop you doing the things that you want. Don't let it make you a victim for the rest of your life. Get the people that you need around you to support you, accept that you cannot change what happened in the past, but you can certainly change what happens in the future.

Use the words "How could I....?" a lot. Instead of thinking how bad things are, look for ways to improve them. Approach everything with a problem-solving frame of mind. Incorporate the biological changes that we spoke about in the last chapter, and the social changes that we will look at in the next one, and then go back to look at the problem again.

You must also understand your rules. These are the things that you think 'should' be done, your right and your wrong. If you are constantly going against your own rules, you will not be happy. Maybe your rules just exist because of a false belief (such as, rich people are unethical, and I don't want to be unethical).

Your rules can be much more far-reaching than you realize. One of the main areas in your life that these can affect is your relationships with other people.

For example, if your rules tell you that if your husband does not hug you and speak to you the moment he walks through the door, then he does not love you, then you will have problems if you have a husband who heads straight for coffee when he comes in. That does not mean that he does not love you, it means that he does not have the same rules as you for what is needed for 'love'. If your boss upsets you by being abrupt, that doesn't mean he doesn't respect you, it means that he has different rules around how you should speak to other people. He maybe thinks that this is how managers 'should' act.

Remember, emotion comes from the meaning that you give something, not from the thing itself. If your relationship with someone is difficult, try to understand the rules that they are following. If it's a close relationship, speak to the other person about how it makes you feel when they do a certain thing, and try to find a way that works for both of you. But never forget that it you can change the meaning, you can change the emotion – and a negative meaning will always bring about a negative emotion.

One last word here on the subject of emotions and feelings. All feelings are *real* – yours and other people's. If you feel it, or they feel it, it's real, because it's what is personally experienced. Whether other people may find it childish, or petty, or downright silly, it's real if it's real to you. Never try to tell yourself that your feelings are stupid. That will only hurt you and cause you pain and confusion. Instead, be patient with yourself, acknowledge how you feel, and then ask yourself how else you could feel. You have choices. You have control. Use it to your advantage to find more helpful emotions. Do things that make you feel better, start to think in such a way as to make you feel more hopeful, more positive, more in control.

Your mind is the most fantastic, powerful machine, which can work either for you or against you. If you can take the time to understand it and work with it to bring about positive changes, you will have the ability to radically alter your life.

14 SOCIAL ENVIRONMENT

Social conditioning is often ignored as a factor in people's development, self-concept and ways of thinking. However, I have realized, after years of people telling me where they feel their issues lie, that the influence that this can have on your views is highly underrated.

As we have spoken about previously, people use categorization to help them to make sense of other people and of events. They also use categorization to make sense of themselves. The categories, which are known as schemas, are used to store all of the information that we have compiled.

Schema development starts very early in life, and continues throughout it. Although the information in our schemas is influenced by our internal mechanisms (our psychological and biological differences) it is also strongly influenced by external influences – that is, the social and cultural setting in which we are growing up.

It is believed that our self-concept develops by the studying the people around us, and taking in (or "internalizing") the products of our interactions with them. By this, we mean that we absorb and take on the values and beliefs of those around us. Think back to the people who surrounded you when you were a child, especially those that you looked up to. Parents are usually a very important source of information, but we also learn from others – teachers, siblings, peers – and from third party sources like TV programs and the news. From all of these sources we build up a picture of what 'me' is.

Some of the parts that make up 'me' are fairly indisputable, such as race and gender. Others are less so, but we can learn to take them as just as much of a fact. For instance, if a number of people tell you that you are disorganized, you may start to believe that. The amount of people who tell you a 'fact' about yourself, and the faith that you have in their judgment, will influence how likely you are to believe this, and to internalize it as an aspect of 'me'. When you look at yourself and the beliefs that you hold about your character and abilities, you may not realize that many of them are the beliefs of other people that you have taken onboard.

'Me', then, comes from a number of sources.

The first source is the people around you. If you had a loving, supportive family, who helped you to grow as a person, and gave you the confidence to explore, knowing that they would be there to help you if you made mistakes, then you began life with a huge advantage. Humans are social creatures; having good early relationships is a really solid basis for learning how to interact with other people.

Unfortunately, not everyone has this. Some children, growing up in an abusive or neglectful home environment, do not learn good things about relationships. This can influence you in later life. Those who learned that people are generally kind and helpful, and who have that family support network to fall back on, usually find it easier to form relationships later in life. They learn a whole lot of different messages about 'me', and their value in the eyes of other people. Those who had a bad start in life often have to overcome low self-esteem, and difficulties in trusting or even interacting with people.

The second source of 'me' is the groups that you feel that you belong to. The earliest groups are usually race, gender and social class. Our minds work in such a way that these can be thought of as labels that we put on ourselves, and we identify ourselves with those labels. It has been found that the more of a minority group we are considered to belong to, the more strongly we identify with those labels. A white, middle-class man is more likely to identify himself as just a 'person', whereas a black woman from a poor background would be more likely to identify herself as a 'poor black woman'.

We don't know yet exactly why this is, but various

studies have been carried out that produced evidence supporting this. With that in mind, it's worth thinking about what labels you have put on yourself, and if there's anything in them that does not work for you. How do you think about yourself? How do you speak about yourself to other people?

You will learn other identifications as you go through life for the groups that you feel you belong in – athlete, academic, popular, sociable, organized, ambitious, capable.... You will have an idea of some of the labels that you apply to yourself from the notes that you made earlier in the book. Again, it's worth looking closely at these to see if any of them don't work for you, as the person that you want to be. Your views of yourself very strongly affect the confidence you have in your ability to achieve your goals.

The third source of 'me' is the cultural context in which you grew up. Different cultures have very different values for the roles of men and women in society and how relationships between them should work, very different work ethics, very different views on wealth, and what good manners should be, and how people should speak to each other. Your culture, and the society that you witness around you, has a very strong influence on what you believe to be the 'correct' way of behaving. Also be aware that you can have multiple cultural influences – if you grew up in one culture, with a family from another culture, this can create difficulties for you in areas where they conflict on what is 'correct'.

Take a moment to think about all of these different influences that you experienced while growing up, and to understand what you have learned from them about yourself – your identity, your role in life, and how you should behave.

Now we will move on to looking at some of the issues that this social conditioning can cause us. You may not even be aware of them at a conscious level, but the beliefs that you have taken in about yourself affect you all the time, influencing both the way that you view things and the way that you emotionally experience them.

If you did not receive the love and support that you should have had while you were growing up, you might, along with many others, have taken this to mean that you were not deserving of love, or of support. This is very sad, but unfortunately it happens a lot. When we are young, we are very vulnerable to the actions of other people, and to believing that what we get is what we deserve. I see so many people in pain, through no fault of their own, because they have been made to feel unloved, or unwanted, or useless.

Let me tell you something about the power of 'I'. You have the ability, if you let yourself, to reject the labels that other people have put on you, and to be what *you* want to be, not what they have made you. If you are angry, or hurt, by how people have treated you, recognize that holding onto the anger and hurt does not harm anyone but you. Learn to let it go. Also, learn to assign the fault where it belongs – to the people who did not treat you as you deserved. Whether this was bad parents, an unkind teacher, bullies at school – let it go. Accept that it happened, and walk past it. Do you want your own life, or the life that other people have put you into? 'I' has the power to do that. 'I' is your conscious awareness.

Look at it this way. 'I' is how you really feel – the true you. 'Me' is other people's perceptions, which you have taken on. To understand 'me', you need to be able to step into someone else's shoes and look at yourself through their eyes. Why did they say the things that they did to you, act in the way that they did? Maybe you did something to upset them. Maybe they were just thoughtless. Maybe you inconvenienced them in some way. People have any number of reasons for saying and doing the things that they do, but this doesn't make their beliefs a fact, and it does not have to control how you think about yourself. If you look at things from their point of view, understand why they acted as they did, and find something in yourself that you don't like, change it. If you don't agree with their opinion, reject it!

Whether you believe it yet or not, you are a marvelous creation. Each human being is totally unique and has the ability to go out and change their life. Learn to love yourself. Another person's opinion does not define you.

Your social group identifications can also cause issues for you. What happens if you define yourself as something unhelpful? What did you write down about yourself at the beginning of this book?

Think back to the section on affirmations. Say, for example. that you want to be a millionaire. You can make numerous affirmations stating that you are a millionaire, that you live in a mansion, drive a Bentley, own a yacht. You can set all of your goals correctly, write them down, express them exactly – "I have £5,000,000 in the bank – and nothing happens. Why? Some would say that it's because you didn't take the actions you needed to get that (and of course, you need to take action to get anything that you want!) but it can be a deeper problem than that.

Your identity is defined by your past and your current perceptions. You may identify yourself as something unhelpful – a gang member, a criminal, poor, of a low social group. All the money in the world will not change this perception. The only thing that will change this perception is for you to take control of your conscious mind and to refuse to be defined by what you have experienced, and where you are now. The chances are that if you won the lottery tomorrow, it wouldn't really change how you feel about yourself. You would just be a luckier, wealthier version of whoever you are today.

Change comes from the inside, on all levels. The start of any change is a conscious decision to make it, and then an action plan to bring it into being. If you want to change who you are, you need to change the way that you think about yourself.

Always remember that you have the power to do something different – there are always choices. While you may have had a worse start in life than others, while you might have done things in the past that you regret, tomorrow is always another day. If you are having trouble moving forward, you may need to change your labels.

Your behavior and feelings are triggered by the way that you interact with people. If you don't like your interactions, change your behaviors and feelings. A huge part of the human experience is based on our relationships with other people, so it is critical to make sure that you act in such a way as to make these pleasant for you.

Say, for example, that you have done time in prison. If you are still identifying yourself with this label, it may affect the way that you expect people to deal with you. The fact that the other person might not even know about it does not matter. Your 'I' has expectations about what the other person will feed back to you as 'Me', and you will act accordingly.

Think about perception. We see, to a certain extent, what we expect. If the other person is abrupt with you and ends the conversation, you may believe that this is the other person judging you, because you are an ex-prisoner. In reality, you might be expecting a rejection, and projecting hostility, defensiveness or dislike, and this may be what the person is walking away from.

If you are mixing with a room of really wealthy people, and you came from a poor background, again you may project a host of negative emotions which makes people avoid you. You will perceive their reaction to be one of snobbishness, and this will reinforce your belief that wealthy people do not want to speak to you. Remember classical conditioning? You will learn to associate meeting rich people with rejection and discomfort, and this will reinforce your self-stereotype that you're not the sort of person who can move in those circles.

IT'S ALL IN YOUR MIND

(One note here. Yes, there are people in the world who judge others based on gender, skin color, social group, appearance, and other factors which have no bearing at all on how nice a human being you are. Don't even think for a moment before rejecting the views of these people. Why would you want to take on board anything that an ignorant bigot says? And if they are judging you based on something so superficial, do you really think that opinion has any merit?)

If you want to change the nature of your relationships with people, learn to break the cycle. Meet people with an open mind. Change the way that you react. This does not mean that you have to change you, your core personality, just to please others. Speech, clothes, image are just tools that you can use, they don't need to define you. The only thing that really defines you is the way that you think about yourself, and the person that you decide to be.

Be aware that you will always present yourself differently to different people – you behave differently with your boss and your kids, with your wife and with your parents. That doesn't mean you have more than one personality. It just means that you behave differently in different situations.

Language – verbal and non-verbal – is an important tool in every one of your interactions. The problem with language is that we can only use what we have learned.

If you came from a very violent background, you won't get the experience of how to speak to people in a kind, gentle manner – in an environment where this might be considered as weakness, you probably won't see it at all. Remember, language is a tool, like any other. If you wanted to build a fence, you would find a hammer. If you want to build good social relationships, find the spoken and body language that will help you to do that. There are examples all around us. Find someone that you admire, and see what you admire about them. Then try it out for size. You don't just need to internalize what other people give you. You can decide what to internalize for yourself.

It's also true that by nature we are inclined to maximize our similarities with others that we perceive to be in the same group, and maximize our differences from those in other groups. This, unfortunately, is the basis of discrimination and hatred of people based on class, race or sexuality. Humans are inclined to subconsciously fear what is different, and to increase their feelings of security with group membership. This does not help when you are trying to move away from a label that you have taken upon yourself.

At the end of the day, we are all humans. Moving in and out of groups is possible, and much of the time happens naturally through the course of our lives. However, we can be wary of making the conscious decision to move to what we consider a "higher" group, due to fear of stigma and fear of rejection. Always remember that groups are a social construct, they are not usually defined boundaries of what you have to be. Fear and lack of self-belief can prevent change.

It's also known that people can find the idea of leaving groups really painful, and not only because this may be moving out of their comfort zone. There can be guilt at the thought of wanting to leave the group. Also, if you think about it, this is a challenge to your identity. If you have very strongly internalized your membership of that group, it has become a part of you. We instinctively fear losing our identity. Keep in mind though that if you do not want to stay in a certain place, you don't have to. Just be aware that any feelings of fear at making change can be based in this instinctive reaction.

Cultural stereotyping is another problem in that you are exposed, from a young age, to ideas of what you are "supposed" to be like. This can cause real issues for you if it clashes with what you want to be, and your ideas of yourself.

As a very business and career oriented woman who

grew up in a family culture where it was felt that women should marry, have children and keep the house tidy, I can sympathize with this to a great degree. I took the path of going the other way, focusing totally on career and independence, until I had a very unbalanced life where my career dominated everything. It took me until the age of 25, when I married my husband, to find a balance.

People can find themselves either trapped in the cultural 'rules' of their childhood, or going in completely the opposite direction to prove that they are not controlled by those rules. Neither side gives balance. Ask yourself what you have taken in about your role in society from the culture that you grew up in. Is this congruent with the things that you want to do?

Social stereotypes must necessarily cause conflict on a social level, where they are incongruent with our goals or personal feelings. In order to be able to go on and do the things you want, you need to make your peace with those feelings. Accept that this is what society and your culture believes, but that your rules are different. You need above all to be true to yourself. If you find that you are personally happy that there is nothing morally or ethically wrong with the things that you want, then do not let other people's beliefs stop you. This does not mean that you are showing disrespect for your culture, it means that you are accepting that this is the way it is, but that you cannot be happy if you allow it to stand in the way of your vision.

It is critical when looking at all of your socially conceived ideas about yourself and about how you should behave that you understand them and accept them when you are making decisions about change. If you do not know where the problems lie, how can you go about fixing them? Allow yourself enough time to really think about your view of yourself as a person now, and your view of yourself as the person you want to be. Your social identity affects your self-esteem and your beliefs around what you can accomplish. Never forget that we are all people. I would make a bet that there is something that you can do that I can't do. Something you can do that your hero can't do. We are far too fond of putting ourselves down and holding ourselves back. Look at your talents and your good qualities, rather than focusing on your disadvantages.

If human development is an end result of your biology, thought processes and social conditioning, it follows that changing any one of these three things will have an effect on the other two. What you are can never be permanently defined, one of our greatest gifts is the ability to make changes. Looking at this from a social perspective, you must understand that you are not your childhood, or your past or current social environment, although these will have influenced your development as a person. You are a unique human being, with the ability to remove labels that are holding you back, and to choose ones that will take you where you want to go. Have faith in your own abilities and confidence that you will succeed, and you will find that 'I' can overwrite the 'me' that you have learned.

15 USE OF IDENTITIES

The combination of your biology, thought processes and social environment, then, has brought you to be the person that you are today. You are a product of these things, all combined to make a single, core personality. Overlaid on top of that core personality is a set of identities that you use in your day to day interactions with other people, the roles that you have in different aspects of your life.

You will understand by now that you are not a fixed person, trapped in the personalities and identities that you have today. You have the capacity to grow, and to change. You would do this naturally, when events came along that forced you to reassess who you were and what you were capable of. We learn by our responses to new situations, discovering more about ourselves and our abilities. How we react to the things life throws at us is part of what helps us to define who and what we are – our strengths and weaknesses, our feelings and beliefs. Everything that has happened during your life has left some sort of mark on your character, for good or for bad. Everything that happens in the future will also do that.

Given, then, that we will change anyway, does it not make sense to control that change, to make it happen in a way that works for you?

Some people fear change. This is a fairly natural human reaction, but think about this a little more closely. If you fear change, why? If the change was going to be that someone you really cared about fell in love with you, or that you got a much better job, or that suddenly you had a lovely new car because you won a prize draw, or you lost the weight that you wanted to lose, would you fear those changes? Of course not, you would welcome them. It follows then that if we fear change, it's because we don't know how that change will affect us, and we fear that it will be *bad*.

Think about that for a moment. If you are afraid of something changing, what are you afraid of? There is no logical reason for change itself to be bad – change just is. Everything changes, on a small to a great level, from the cells in your body to the condition of the earth. If you fear change, you are failing to deal with something that will happen every day. This is not something which is helpful to you. Instead of fearing that things will change, embrace that, but determine that they are going to change for the *better*.

This brings me back, yet again, to the issue of control. In addition to fearing that change will be bad, we fear that we will not be able to control it. How would you feel if you acknowledged that change was going to come, but that when this happened, you would be ready for it, armed with the knowledge and courage that you needed to control what happened to you? That, whatever happened, you would be able to deal with it?

Can you see that what humans think of as fear of change, which is the basis of people's natural reaction of resistance to change, is actually a combination of two things - fear of something happening that will make their situation worse, and fear that when this happens, they will not be able to control it?

Change will happen to you anyway, it is inevitable. Given that you cannot prevent this, does it not make sense to make sure that change is something that you bring about, rather than something that happens to you?

To do this, you need to understand two things. Firstly, you need to understand the things that you want to change. Secondly, you need to understand the person that you will have to be to bring those changes about.

To understand what you want to change, look back to the beginning of this book, where you wrote down your goals. Pick the one that is most important to you. Begin to imagine what your life would be like if you achieved this goal. What would be different? Picture this in great detail. Take as much time as you need. Imagine all the details.

Once you have this really clearly in your mind, start to think about how you would feel if that goal was achieved. Imagine that you have stepped into your body at that point in time. What emotions are you experiencing? What accomplishments have you got that made you able to bring these things about? What is different to how you are now?

Doing this will give you an understanding of a very powerful tool that you can use to bring about transformation in your own life. This tool is called modeling.

Modeling will be a familiar concept to many people reading this book, but I want to go into this in more detail, because I use it slightly differently to many other authors. To me, modeling is not just about looking at traits that other people have. It's about absorbing them into yourself to build, effectively, a composite identity designed for the particular goal or position that you have in mind, and then learning to feel and experience it to the point that it becomes second nature.

If you have seen the film *Avatar*, this will help to give you an insight into what I mean. The main character is put into a constructed body resembling that of the natives of the planet that he is on, and ends up living with the native people. In the beginning, he tries to act like one of their community, but because he does not really understand who they are and how they think, this is difficult for him, and he makes a lot of mistakes. He may look like one of them, but inside, he is still his human self. Over time, from living with them and beginning to understand their values and their abilities, he begins to respect and admire them, to absorb their beliefs and to emulate their behavior. After a while, he starts to become the thing that he looks like, rather than a body in an avatar.

The key steps of modeling are all in there. First, there is an understanding of what you want to be. Next, there is observation of the abilities and beliefs that this person would need. Next, there is modeling – not just copying a trait or behavior, but living the person that you want to be. Finally, you reach the point where you are no longer modeling. You have made these traits and abilities your own.

Some people find the thought of doing this frightening, as if it can somehow threaten their own personality, or as if the end result will be multiple different personalities. As I said in an earlier chapter, personality and identities are a very different thing. You may change your core personality, but only by giving it more helpful traits and supportive emotional responses – things that will help you. Your core personality will still be you – the changes that you make just help you to be the person that you want to be, with more control over your life and more choices. Your identities will help you to get the things that you want in life, and with use, the helpful aspects of each identity will be absorbed into your core personality. The rest will stay with that identity, useful for that role in your life, but maybe not so useful in others.

When I was in my late teens, I developed quite a distinctive dress style – lots of black clothes, lots of black make-up, big boots, big hair. As I've mentioned in the social chapter, we can identify very strongly with certain groups, and are more likely to do so if the group we are in is considered a minority. I was rather fond of my new identity, and saw it as a way of expressing myself. Unfortunately, as I was working in a bank at the time, my employers were nowhere near so fond of it. I saw their disapproval as a challenge to my self-expression. They saw my dress sense as a disregard for their culture.

One day, I was complaining about this to Gill, my aunt, and she said something which has stuck with me throughout life. What she said was, "But why does it matter? Dress how they want you to at work if it will get you what you want. You can take it off when you come home, and dress however you like."

The point is this: sometimes in life, we have to make sacrifices to achieve the things that we want. However, doing something during your working day does not mean that you have to bring it home with you. Nothing affects your core personality unless you decide to take it on-board and internalize it into your beliefs. Changing my way of dressing for work did not make any change to my core personality, it merely changed my identity at work. Three weeks later, now that people were looking at my abilities rather than my weird hair, I got a promotion.

Remember, it's not what happens that has an effect, it's the meaning that we give it. I stopped seeing the dress code at work as something that was there to stop me being myself, and accepted it instead as something that was just a fact of life. Once I had taken out the meaning that this was a threat to my personality, it wasn't a problem to wear suits. At the weekend, I wore whatever I wanted, and during the week I got paid more for doing something I liked better.

I had never heard of modeling then, but I had learned an important principle. What you project on the outside is what people will believe about you. Whether that's clothes, intelligence, personality – people will make their judgments about you based on what they see. It doesn't matter if you're a lovely person with a high IQ – if the face you show to the world is one that's unfriendly and disinterested, that's what people will respond to.

If you think that this makes you somehow not "You", remember that everything you are, you have modeled. You have been modeling since you were a very young child, internalizing other people's beliefs, and the things that they have said about you which you have built into the concept of "Me". You are going to model anyway, so why not do it to your advantage?

Firstly, you need to learn how to reject the aspects of "Me" that other people have forced on you. These are not set in stone – they are open to disagreement! Far too many people accept the things that people have told them about their lack of skill, intelligence, beauty, social skills. If you do not like it, refuse to accept it, and change what you need to. Only you can do this, and you do have the power to do it, if you put your mind to it.

As we said earlier, the things that you modeled when you were growing up were restricted by the environment that you grew up in. A child growing up in an environment of bad language will think that everyone swears. A child growing up with violence will believe that everyone suffers violence. A child growing up in an environment of multiple generation welfare dependency will see this as the normal way of living. If you lived in a war zone, where bombs were falling every day, as a child, this would just be how things were.

As we get older, our ability to challenge the status quo grows as our cognitive processes develop, but we do not always choose to do so. Many people believe that, as it has always been, so it will always be, and that they cannot change this. The process of change begins with belief – your own belief that you are not limited by the things that you have experienced in the past, and that you can make a conscious choice to bring about a change. Once you start to challenge the things that your environment has imposed on you, you begin to acquire the control that you need to change them.

First of all, make an effort to understand what exactly it is that you want to be. It doesn't matter if this is a specific kind of person with regard to certain character traits, or a specific career role or business role, the principle is the same. You need to be able to understand that and to create that person within yourself.

I want you to sit down and clearly think about what that person would be like. Make sure that you are in a quiet room where you won't be disturbed. Get a pen and write down everything that you can think of about that person (writing things down, in your own words, helps you to code that information in your head).

I want you to think very carefully about every aspect of that person. What would a ………….. look like? How would they think? How would they feel? How would they speak? How would they react to people? How would they feel when they got out of bed in a morning? How would they look forward to the day ahead? How would they plan for the things that they had to do? How would they cope with a crisis?

Next, I want you to think about what that person would need to know. What qualifications would they need to have? What experience? What career skills? What soft skills, such as time management or people management? What people would they need to have around them as a power team?

Now read back through the notes that you have made and get a very clear idea inside your head of everything that this person is. How do the skills that you have relate to this? You should have two distinct pieces of information from this exercise. One is the things that you need to know – academic or skills training knowledge, and the partners or the supporting experts that you would need to have around you. There is no shortcut to this – you need to go out there and do your research. The Internet has changed the world in terms of the ease of access of information. Buy books, take courses, join a networking group – do whatever you need to do to acquire the right skills and the right people around you.

The other thing that you need is a specific set of character traits that you need to have, and may not have already. This is where modeling comes in.

The traits that you need are out there – someone, without a doubt, already has them. You need to find them, and you need to model them. It doesn't matter if they are a real person or not – it can be an actor playing a role in a film or TV program, so long as this conveys to you the trait that you need to model.

Bear in mind, too, that you don't need to model just one person. The real question here is what do you need, and who has it? You can pick one person for their dress sense, another for their financial ability, another for their humanity, another for their assertiveness, another for their perseverance in the face of adversity. There is no limit to this. Be like a kid in a sweet shop. Look for every single trait that you feel you need, and then look for the person who best represents this to you.

Now you must do the final step, and put it all together. The question that you need to ask yourself here is, how would *I* feel as that person?

To do this, stand up, take a deep breath, and relax. Imagine a space in front of you, into which you will project all of the things that you need. Now imagine that you have all of those things. Run through the people in your head, visualize them doing one of the things that makes you feel that they are in possession of that attribute that you want. Into that space in front of you, project your belief that you can do and have these things. Don't just imagine it – feel it! The more energy you can put into your visualization, the more that you can actually feel and experience it, the stronger the coding will be that puts these things into your mind as an available resource. Remember biopsychosocial. You must experience this on all levels – how you would physically look and feel, how you would think, and how the people around you would behave towards you, and how you would behave towards them.

Take your time. When you can really see and feel it, step forward into the space where you visualized everything and projected your energy. Take a deep breath. Experience what you have created. How does it feel? How do *you* feel as a person with all of those attributes?

This may seem simple. Actually, it is simple. Don't be fooled into thinking that because something is simple, it

IT'S ALL IN YOUR MIND

does not work. The subconscious itself is very simple. You give it information, it takes it in. The conscious mind is a lot more complex, but at the end of the day, really it's just like a computer. You may think that computers are brilliant, but they can only run with the code that you give them. If you want them to perform a function, they are limited by their available software. If you don't have the code to run that function, the computer can't do it. And if you don't have the code to run a function in your mind, your mind can't do it. What you are doing here is giving yourself code to use for new functions, and data for that code to work on. The things that make you a unique human being, your feelings and emotional responses, all arise from that software and that data. To change your experience, you need to change the data and change the code.

Remember, you are not modeling a person. It's far better to be a unique you than a copy of someone else! What you are modeling is aspects of that person which are more useful to you than the ones that you have now, and you are incorporating them into your identity. Identity is a resource that you can use in your interactions. Learn to use it to your advantage. It's a set of traits which are required for a specific role. You can have multiple roles, all with different traits to support them. You can also use this technique to take in traits that you want to be part of your core self, like compassion, or confidence, or patience.

Who remembers Worzel Gummidge? For those who have never seen this TV program, Worzel was a scarecrow who changed his heads. He had different heads for different abilities – he had, for example, a clever head. When he needed to be clever, he used that head. When he didn't, he used another one. Identities, in the same way, are a resource pool that you can draw on. You don't need to wear them all the time.

Of course, some identities are not open to choice. Your race, your gender, any disability, for example, are parts of you that you cannot change with simple visualization. Learning to accept what you cannot change is a key step to a peaceful mind. However, also be aware that these too are only aspects of your identity. They do not define you. Nothing, in fact, should define you – you should define yourself. You are not a victim of circumstance, you have choices and you have the control to make them.

If you think that creating identities is strange, be aware that we do this constantly in our conversations with other people. Humans negotiate for position all the time in their conversations.

Think about how you would position yourself as, for example, a good dad. You have an idea in your head about what a good dad would behave like – this is a discourse, that is, your own story about what makes a good dad. In the positions you negotiate with other people, if you are convincing them that you are a good dad, you will refer to this discourse to provide the information that you need to do so, and you will speak in such a way as to negotiate the position that you match these criteria. You are negotiating all the time, in conversations with your parents, your kids, your partner, your boss, your bank manager. This is how we work. And now, using the techniques above, you are negotiating with yourself.

If you're a skeptic, you're probably doubting this, because we're not always aware that we do it. Think about this example. One person that you work with will probably say that everyone at the company is lovely, that the boss is really supportive, and the environment is pleasant. Someone else will say that everyone at the company is moody, the boss is a bully, and that the work environment makes them miserable. How can this be true? Well, it can be true that both people really believe their own version. This is because we position other people, and how we position them changes our expectations, which in turn changes what we see and experience. This is why some people think everyone is nice, and some people think everyone is mean!

One final point about discourses. Remember that they are interactive – the people that you speak to will be constructing their views of you based on your interactions with them, so think carefully about what you are saying to people! Also, try to put yourself in the other person's shoes – another fairly unique human ability – use it to understand what the other person actually feels and wants, rather than just listening to what they are saying, or watching what they are doing. People don't always put what they want and how they feel into words very well – sometimes they don't even realize what that is themselves. A very important part of being the person that you want to be is understanding how you need to speak to people, and how your discourses can affect both how you see other people, and how they see you.

Now that we are getting towards the final stages of the book, we're going to go back and run through the steps to making these changes in your mind that are needed to bring about the changes that you are looking for in your life. Before we do so, though, I am going to run through the two bugs in the machine which, if you're not aware of them can cause all of your carefully laid plans to fall apart. These bugs are called negative emotions and secondary gain. In the next two chapters, we will look at what these are, how they affect us, and why it is so important that we understand and control them.

16 NEGATIVE EMOTIONS

Every human being, at some time or other in their life, suffers from negative emotions. It's not possible that everything that we experience will be positive. Bereavement, the end of a relationship, financial loss, betrayal of trust, disappointment, and a host of other things that we do not want: at some stage, one or more of these things will affect all of us. It's unrealistic to expect that life will always be sunshine and roses; indeed, if it was, we would never be able to fully appreciate the pleasure that we feel when things are going well. There's no day without night, and there's no joy without pain. Our experiences are comparative.

It's also unrealistic to expect that, having experienced a traumatic or tragic event, we will not feel a negative response. Learning to control your emotions and your responses cannot prevent you feeling some sort of painful reaction after a distressing event. Indeed, it is not healthy to try to suppress all negative emotions. They are a natural response, and we have them for a reason. They provide an outlet for the pain, and a way of expressing how we feel about it.

The problem with negative emotions comes when we let them affect the functioning of our lives, and when they impact upon all of our reactions, all of our thoughts, intrusively, and in a way that is not beneficial to us. If you let them control you, negative emotions will eat you up from the inside. If you are not aware of them, and don't take action to make sure that they are not ruling all of your responses, you won't be able to react in the way that you want to react, in order to get the things that you want to get.

We are going to look at a few of the most common negative responses that I have encountered over the years, the reasons we may have them, and the more positive emotions and goals that we can use to counter them.

ANGER

I've already mentioned anger in a previous chapter, but I will mention it again, because of all the emotions that I have seen affecting people, this is probably both the most prolific, and the most damaging.

Lots of people are angry. They are angry with their parents for neglecting them, with their partner for leaving them, with their friend for letting them down, with their boss for sacking them. They are angry with the government, the law, the economy, God, life, the universe and everything. Do you know someone like this? There are a lot of people who just seem to be angry all of the time.

Have you seen what happens when rust gets inside the wheel arch of a car? The first thing you see is a tiny orange spot. If you don't do something about it, it spreads, and it spreads quickly. Soon, previously solid metal is bubbling and full of holes. Anger, like rust, is a corrosion.

The problem with angry people is that anger becomes a habit. They begin to expect that others will say or do something to make them angry. If you remember the cognitive section, you'll know that we often see what we expect to see. Therefore, angry people see and experience a lot to make them angry. Some of these things would cause most people to shake their head or shrug their shoulders and walk away.

Anger, however, is a hot emotion. People who are experiencing it often don't have the detachment to realize that the other person may be annoying, but not enough for them to feel this sense of rage. Angry people often project the justifiable anger that they feel towards one person, who may not be around any more to be the target of that anger, onto someone else. Often, they don't even realize that this is what they are doing. The anger feels real, and the target of it seems to be deserving of it.

Do you remember the quote that I gave you about anger? Anger is like drinking poison and expecting the other person to die.

That quote made a huge impact on me when I first heard it; in fact, in the list of things that I have been told over the course of my life, that's well up on the scale of life-changing events. I spent a lot of years angry, and by being focused on my own anger, I missed out on a lot of opportunities because I was busy being mad. When you are focusing on anger, you are not focusing on contentment, joy, or success. These emotions don't exist well with anger. Anger stifles them.

There may be people in your life who have done terrible things to you, cost you your health or your happiness, and inflicted a lot of pain on you. You need to let this go and walk away. I am not in any sense telling you to forgive them because we need to love everyone, because they too are a human being, because they had their own problems, they are not well.... I am telling you to forgive them because your anger is not hurting them, it's hurting you. I'm also not telling you that you need to have them back in your life. Maybe they are genuinely sorry. Maybe they don't understand, or don't care what they did. What you choose to do about that person in the future is your own decision, and you have a responsibility to yourself to make it in your own interest. What I am telling you to do is to draw a line, and start looking forward rather than looking back.

The person or persons with whom you are angry may not even know that you feel this way towards them any more. If they did know, they might even get some sense of satisfaction that they are still so important in your life. Why would you want to invest so much emotional intensity in someone who has wronged you? Save your emotional intensity for those whom you love, and who love you.

Anger will make you ill and burn you out. It will get in the way of your future happiness and prevent you getting real enjoyment out of life. Make the decision, right now, to let it go. Don't allow it to be so important to you. Accept what happened, and then leave it behind you. You deserve a happy future, unburdened by such a destructive emotion. If you are still holding onto anger, put it to rest right now.

GUILT

Guilt is an emotion that cripples ambition and takes the pleasure out of life. Regret and guilt are very different emotions. Regret acknowledges that we wish we had not done something, and would take it back if we could. Guilt focuses you on the pain and discomfort which is linked in your mind with the action.

I have seen, on many occasions, that people who are deeply guilty about something have a desire to punish themselves. They also have a tendency to feel that this guilt makes them an unworthy person, someone who is not deserving of success, or happiness. Guilt taken too far can lead to deep depression, and loss of self-esteem.

If you are suffering under a burden of guilt, take a moment to think who that guilt actually benefits? The truth is that guilt, held too long, benefits nobody.

Guilt is an unhelpful emotion. If your guilt is based on something that you did to someone, how can it help them? Of course, it cannot. Feeling guilty is not doing a single thing towards putting right what you did, it's just draining your energy into a bottomless pit.

Guilt, when one realizes that they have done something wrong, is a natural response. At this time, acknowledge that you should not have said, or done, whatever it is, and take the lesson from that. Resolve never to repeat it.

Guilt is a useful tool for registering inside your head that to do this thing is wrong; next time you may be about to do something similar, alarm bells will go off, and you will think back to the previous occasion and how you felt at that time. That should be enough to prevent you from repeating your mistake. However, guilt is not a stick to hit yourself over the head with. We all do things that we regret later. If you focus only on the mistake, you're not focusing on what you could have done instead, and making that the thing that you would do next time.

The best way to make up for things that you have done in the past is to go out now and do something good for someone. Maybe you can do something to help the person that you hurt, but maybe you cannot. If not, there are plenty of other people that you can help. Give money or time to help a charity, assist an elderly neighbor, help out in your community, try to give some kids a better start than you had. It doesn't really matter what it is, so long as you are focused on the fact that to help people is good. Isn't that more productive than sitting around thinking how bad a person you must be? Also, doing things for other people, for love of helping them rather than looking for a reward, is immensely satisfying. That has to be a win-win situation.

At the extreme ends of guilt, I have spoken to people who have had troubled lives – people who have spent time in children's homes, in prisons, and in gangs. Very often, they are stuck in this persona, unable to move away from it, and full of guilt for their past actions. There are two things that I try to help them to understand.

Think back to the social chapter, and what we discussed there. The first issue that people have is with their environment, and what they grow up believing is the 'norm'. When they later move on in life, they experience issues on two levels. Perhaps their environment has changed, and they now see their past actions are terrible, even though at the time this was what was available to them. Perhaps they want to move on, but are stuck in that environment. Also, however much you feel that you don't want to be in that place any more, you can actually experience guilt at wanting to leave it. This is part of the programming that tells us that there is safety in numbers, and that we need to be part of a group – and which therefore makes us maximize our similarities with one group, and our differences with "outsiders".

The second issue that they have is that it has affected their self-concept (remember that we have schemas that hold information about ourselves, as well as schemas about other things and people). Their schema tells them that they are a bad person, and they are trapped in that identity.

Always remember that people make the best choices that they can at the time. There's no reason for us to do anything else, is there? So we must make what seem like the right choices *at that moment*, based on the information that we have, and our emotional state.

What you did at that time, as that person, is obviously different from what you would do now. If you were still the same person, you would not be torturing yourself with guilt over it. You now have better information and better choices.

Bear in mind, too, that some of the actions that you hate may have been forced upon you – to prevent you showing weakness, or for survival. Do not allow yourself to be stuck in a perceived social group or perceived role. Every person has the ability to move on. Holding onto your guilt does not help with this. Make choices now that you will never do that thing again, focus on the good things that you can do for others instead of the bad things that you have done in the past, and *forgive yourself*.

JEALOUSY

Jealousy is a strange emotion. If you are jealous of

someone, it's usually because they have something that you want, and feel that you can't have. Maybe they are rich, or popular, or lucky, or intelligent. The focus of your emotion is around the thing, although it reflects on the person who has it. Therefore, if you think about it, you are tying up a negative emotion with something that you really want.

Every time that you look at someone and envy them, you are pouring negative energy into the thought of having wealth, or popularity, or luck, or intelligence. The feeling that you get will be a bad one. We've already discussed that human nature is geared to make us move away from things that make us feel bad, and towards things that make us feel good. This is our motivation. If every time you think about being rich, it makes you feel bad, you are unlikely to start taking the actions that you may want to take in order to make more money.

What about trying, instead, to like that thing about them? When you look at them, rather than feeling jealous and bitter, say to yourself "I would love to have *(whatever it is)* and I will have it. What will my life be like when I have that thing? Now picture it. What emotion do you feel now? You probably feel happiness, or excitement.

Learn to recognize when you are feeling jealous, and switch that emotion off immediately. It does not matter if you feel the person isn't deserving of having that thing; whether they are or not is totally irrelevant as to whether or not *you* deserve it.

Personally, I believe that everyone is deserving of anything they are prepared to put the energy in to get, so long as it was ethically gained. Be prepared to put positive energy into the pursuit of what you want, rather than getting caught up in the negative emotion of jealousy towards people who already have it. Being jealous will not help you at all in pursuit of your goals. Focus on what matters – what you are doing.

RESENTMENT

Resentment is my personal favorite. If there was ever an underestimated emotion tied up with holding you back, this is it. Resentment isn't hot, like anger. Resentment is like toothache – it nags and nags, and it's constantly in the back of your mind if you give it room in there. I feel pretty qualified to speak about resentment, as this was always my Achilles heel. I wasn't aware of this until started to get involved in NLP. After that, it probably took all of two hours to find out that pretty much all of the issues that I had were tied up with my own personal pet phrase.

That's not fair.

When you think about it, it's pretty amazing that three short words could make the difference between the life I had then and the life I have now, but I promise you that they did. When I got rid of them, things turned around pretty much overnight. My outlook changed, and everything else changed around it. I had no idea that the way I thought about things had such a huge impact on my life.

When I was a kid, I had a really easy life. In fact, if I'm honest, I was spoilt rotten. I wasn't much into playing with other kids, I spent most of my time with my face in a book, or in my piano keyboard. My teachers loved me – in fact, most adults seemed to love me – and I was the little princess of the family. I was actually less of a brat than I might have been considering, but life was pretty smooth for me.

When I was ten, things changed drastically. I didn't get on too well with my stepfather, for a start. He wasn't amazingly fond of the child prodigy. I also hadn't worked out by that age that sometimes it's better for your social skills to be obliging, rather than to always be right. I was pretty opinionated and smug.

By the time I got to 14, I had discovered teenage

rebellion. My stepfather was extremely strict, and I wasn't allowed to do most of the things that my friends could do. He was also of the opinion (a culture thing) that girls are not cut out for business, careers and education; as I was rather fond of all those things, the whole situation was destined to be a disaster. At the age of 16, I left boarding school half way through my A-levels, and with a University scholarship already on offer, deciding that I wanted to do things my own way and be my own person.

Most people reading this won't be too surprised when I tell them that this was, to put it mildly, a culture shock. I had made a spur of the minute decision to go from doing things the easy way to doing things the hard way. Actually, I don't regret it – I learned an awful lot that has been useful to me in later life. At the time though, I seriously hadn't got a clue what I was doing.

Life was hard! Of course, a lot of the time life *is* hard, but I hadn't expected it to be. I had to go out and get a job, and study to finish my A-levels in my spare time. I couldn't afford to go and do a degree, it took me six years to be able to save up enough to go to University and I still had to work four hours a day on top of a full-time course. I saw my friends getting on well, with full support from their parents, and that didn't feel fair. How come I couldn't have that? How come my nice home life had got wrecked? How come my jobs always bored me silly? None of it was fair.

It's not fair became a habit, and it lasted a long time. I didn't stick to things that just related to me, either. People who were just in the right place at the right time? People who didn't want to work and got everything for free? People who were killed in accidents, got horrible illnesses, or lost everything? Animal experiments, the situation in Tibet, abandoned pets, neglected children …. It wasn't *fair!* I was obsessed with the injustice of the world – with how some people seemed to get everything, and some people seemed to get absolutely nothing.

By this time, I was doing what was considered to be really well. I had a lovely husband and daughter, a fantastic mum and aunt, a wonderful brother and sisters, a successful consultancy, a dream home, a really nice car .... you would think that I would have been happy, and mainly I was, but I was still obsessed with fairness.

Someone fleecing people out of their life savings, making lots of money conning people into buying out-of-date information, people who had treated others badly getting enormous lottery wins ... any of that was enough to stress me for a week. It wasn't fair that anyone "undeserving" should make money, or have huge amounts of luck.

Of course, the truth is that life is not fair. Some people are born with huge advantages, some with huge disadvantages. The secret is not to focus on what you have, or what other people have. It is to focus on doing the best that you can for yourself, and the best that you can to help others. As soon as I changed my way of thinking, my life turned around. It ceased to matter what other people did, what they got, and how they got it. You can only control what you, yourself do. Suddenly I was focused on what I was doing, not what others were doing, and my whole perspective changed.

If resentment of other people seeming to get things without being deserving of them is one of your hang-ups, let it go. What they have or do not have does not affect you in the slightest. Concentrate only on you, and the people that you love, and try to do the best that you can to help everyone have a good and fulfilling life. That's the end of your responsibility. Let the rest go.

There are many, many negative emotions, and I will not run through them all. You get the idea. I would ask you only to be aware of those negative emotions that you are particularly susceptible to, and learn to detect them. You will know how it makes you feel when they spring up. When they do, have a thought to combat them. If you do this often enough, it will become automatic.

One thing I hear a lot is that people use negative emotions to motivate them. Actually, this does work. Living every day with a negative emotion can give you enormous motivation. However, so can wanting something very badly, and that motivation is a lot kinder to your system. If I had to choose between the carrot and the stick, I would choose the carrot every time. You just need to make sure that the carrot is tempting enough!

Let go of feeling sorry for yourself, blaming yourself, being angry at others, or whatever it is that's preventing you from being able to maintain a calm, positive mind. Do you want these emotions to always hold you back? Which would you prefer to be – happy, or sad?

Speaking of which, let's look at the other bug that might be messing up your system. In the next chapter, we are going to talk about secondary gain.

17 SECONDARY GAIN

If you ask someone why they smoke, they may give you one of a number of answers. It keeps them slim. It helps them to relax. It stops them stressing. It gives them an excuse for a break at work. Whatever the reason, it is enough to keep them smoking, regardless of endless health campaigns which tell us that smoking is harmful.

This is secondary gain.

Everything that we do is caused by a motivation. That motivation may be pleasure, or it may be pain. Fairly obviously then, when we do something, it's either because of the pleasure we associate with doing it, or the pain we expect to get from *not* doing it.

Look at the above example of smoking. All of the responses are actually associated with pain – the pain of weight gain, the pain of not being able to relax, the pain of being stressed, the pain of not having a reason to walk away from their desk for five minutes. The pain of giving up smoking is greater than the pleasure associated with not smoking – for example, having more money, losing the smoker's cough – so they smoke on.

If you're asking how the pain of possibly contracting lung cancer and dying younger can possibly not outweigh the pleasure of smoking, it's a good question, but you are making the assumption that motivations are always logical. They are not.

Humans have a convenient habit of acknowledging that bad things happen, but being convinced that they only happen to other people. Remember, it's not the thing itself that causes the emotion, but the meaning that you give it. Smokers don't give smoking the meaning of illness and death, they give it a meaning of pleasure, or removal of the pain of giving up. The health issues are less relevant, because they don't associate them with pain to *themselves.*

Imagine if a trusted source told you that the next time

you smoked a cigarette, it was guaranteed that you would die. If you believed that would be true, do you think you'd give up? Probably. If that same source could convince you that if you threw your current packet of cigarettes away and never smoked again you would win the lottery, do you think you would give up? Again, probably.

Why? Because the motivation to stay alive, or to be instantly rich, would outweigh both the pleasure you associate with smoking, and the pain that you associate with giving up.

Other motivations work in the same way. The problem is that you may not be aware of all of your motivations, or what secondary gain you are getting from the situation that you are in now.

Maybe you think that there's absolutely no reason for you to want things to stay as they are. You may be surprised. Let's take an extreme example.

Say someone is very ill, maybe with a disease that causes them pain, maybe with a long term illness that stops them doing many of the things that they would like to do. Your initial reaction might be that obviously there is no benefit to illness, and no reason at all for that person to wish to stay ill.

Consciously, you may be right. However, imagine that person has friends and family around them that take care of them, and give them huge amounts of love and support. Subconsciously, they might be afraid that, without the illness, they might not receive that level of care; that it is the illness that is the cause of the support, and that without it, they would not receive as much love and attention. What if the pleasure of the care outweighed the pain of the illness?

What about a person who is in prison? Would you imagine that anyone would want to be locked up? However, when you think about it, there are some benefits to the situation. A person in prison does not have to worry about how to pay bills or buy food. He or she does not have to worry about having nowhere to live, nowhere warm to sleep. Educational facilities, counseling and support may be offered. For a long-term inmate, the environment may be more familiar and less frightening than the outside world. If you think that nobody would trade their freedom for a little security, look up the statistics on the amount of people who reoffend immediately after release.

The truth is that most situations, even ones that initially may appear to be totally negative, usually have some positive aspect. If the pleasure associated with the situation outweighs the pain associated with it, you will lack the motivation to change, however much you think you want to. The secondary gain of the situation outweighs the negatives.

If your main motivation for reading this book is that you want to achieve greater success – to make better progress in your career, start or grow your business, or increase your income – you may be able to say, quite confidently, that you totally, absolutely want this. You may think there are no positives in your current situation. Let me give you a few that I have seen when speaking to people who were absolutely sure that success was what they wanted, and had no idea why it continued to elude them.

- I might fail, then I would see myself as a failure.
- I would lose my self confidence if I made a lot of money and then lost it
- If I mess this up, it won't be able to tell myself any more that it was something I *could* have done, I'll have lost that comfort.
- My friends wouldn't like me any more, I wouldn't feel like one of them.
- It might cause arguments within my family
- People might just like me because I would have

lots of money.
- I would not be comfortable mixing with the people I would need to mix with if I was successful.
- There would be lots of stress if I had that much money.
- I would always be tied to my job or business, it would ruin my social life.
- People would always be trying to rip me off.

These points are fairly easy to understand when you think about them, and fairly easy to resolve. If the pain of issues like this outweighs the pleasure you would gain from being whatever you class as "successful", you won't have the motivation to succeed, no matter how much you think you do.

Your goal must have a pleasure level above any associated pain. If your goal does not give you that, you have the wrong goal. To deal with this, think of every bad thing that you can associate with the goal. Then think of the good things. Compare them. Which has the greater pleasure or pain?

It is absolutely critical that you understand any secondary gain that you are attaching to the situation that you are in now. Often, it's a comfort level – your main gain is that you feel secure and safe. Sometimes, security is the worst possible thing that you can need if you want to push yourself, but it's a common human reaction, and lots of people suffer from it.

Sometimes it can go deeper than that. Who out there thinks of themselves as a victim? It doesn't matter what you think you are a victim *of* ...whether it's your parents, someone who did something to you, life itself ... do you think of yourself as a victim of *something?* Do you feel sorry for yourself because you've had bad luck, bad treatment, bad care?

This may come as something of a shock, but there's

actually an obscure sort of comfort in victim mentality. For one thing, it removes the responsibility from your shoulders and onto those of someone or something else. You can tell yourself it's not your fault. Think about the number of people who get together to complain about how awful life is. In some circles, this is the main form of recreation. The best speaker seems to be the person who can take the title for the worst story. The prize is that everyone is going to feel sorry for you and tell you how unlucky you've been.

If you become very successful, and have all the things that other people would like, nobody is going to feel sorry for you. Well, they might if you get hit by a lorry, but for the usual things in life that people complain about, they are really not going to care. In the eyes of many, as a successful person, you have no right to feel sorry for yourself about anything ordinary. Your luck, or skill, or whatever they attribute your success to, will be judged to be more than enough to make up for your daily upsets.

If you get your goal, you need to be prepared to give up your victim mentality. You may not even have thought about this, but trust me, your subconscious knows! You will no longer be able to feel sorry for yourself about how bad life is. You won't be able to expect sympathy from most of the people around you when you lose some money, or a friend lets you down..

If you think there's no secondary gain going on in your life, take a close look at the things that you like to complain about, the things that you talk about to your friends when you're telling them how unlucky you are.

If you lost your job and your house, be aware that if you get a better job and a better house, people will see that as something that shouldn't matter. To you it may still have a big impact, to others you've replaced it with a better version.

If you were a millionaire in your twenties, lost it all, and then became a multi-millionaire in your thirties, do you think anyone is going to commiserate with you for having to go through the trauma of bankruptcy?

Whether or not you are aware of it, there is a sort of cold comfort from feeling like you have nothing. For one thing, if you have nothing, you have nothing to lose – any move that you make is going to be for the better. For another, sympathy is addictive.

If you have got used to being the person that everyone loves, everyone feels sorry for because their life is so hard, and everyone helps out, you're going to lose that. And if that's how you've created yourself in your self-stereotype, it can be hard to throw it off.

I would advise you to sit down very carefully and think of the secondary gain from anything you have at the moment. If there's a thing or a situation that you don't like, and you can't work out why you are stuck in it, then find the thing that makes it attractive to you and then find something that you could replace it with.

Secondary gain lurks everywhere – in smoking, in overeating, in not taking action to achieve the things that you want to do. If you are going to achieve the things that you want to achieve, you need to understand exactly what you are getting out of your current situation, and what you could get instead. Is it worth the trade? Only you can make that call.

18 BEHAVIORS

There is just one more thing that I would like to mention before we move on to the action plan, and that is behaviors.

One of the things that people have asked me in discussing the work that I do is why I do not speak specifically about behavior. In many cases, our behavior is the thing that's causing us all of the problems. We don't like how we respond to certain events and situations, and this is the very thing that we want to change. Why, then, would I not cover how to change behavior?

It's simple. Behavior is a response. It's a response to our biology, our thought processes, our social conditioning. These feed into our emotions, and also into our beliefs via conditioning and stereotyping. Our attitudes are the result of our beliefs and our feelings, and our behavior is the result of our attitudes. Behavior does not make us who we are – it's a product of it.

Think about how we treat an illness. We don't treat the symptom of the illness, we treat the cause. Yes, we might take medicine for the symptoms, such as painkillers and decongestants, but this doesn't cure the illness, it only masks the symptoms. If you have a serious underlying illness which is causing those symptoms, the medicine does nothing for that. As soon as you stop taking it, the symptoms come back.

It's the same way with a behavior. Changing behaviors might work for dogs, but it's not the best approach for people, who have much more sophisticated biology, reasoning processes and social understandings. Yes, you can specifically target and change a behavior, using operant or classical conditioning in much the same way that you use it for animals. This is used very successfully in treating, say, a phobia of spiders. However, in doing this, you are only changing a single response to a single situation. I prefer to use operant and classical conditioning to control simple emotional responses, and a targeted change of physiology, thought processes and social conditioning to change beliefs, attribution of meaning, and underlying emotions.

If you can change both your beliefs and your emotional responses to be more supportive to you, you are no longer changing a single behavior. Instead, you are changing your attitude to the things going on around you, which will affect every single behavior which derives from that attitude.

Changing behaviors and habits is an ongoing struggle, addressing one thing at a time. I don't see the point of making this hard for yourself. I never find there to be a benefit in doing things the difficult and painful way. I want you to get results, and I want you to enjoy what you are doing to get them.

You can understand, after reading this far, how much your self-concept influences how you respond to things – even how you see them – and that this has consequences which spread into all areas of your life, controlling what you feel, how you react, and the meanings that you assign to things. This is inevitable. Curing one behavior will not fix that – in fact, even if you teach yourself to respond in a certain way, if your mind is not completely in agreement with you that this is the correct response, it won't feel right to you. You may even feel a negative reaction within both your body and your mind – I'm sure you know the feeling that I mean. The one that happens just before you do something that you're not sure is the right thing to do.

If you want to do something with your behaviors, why not take a look at the ones that cause you problems and work your way back up the tree to find out why you behave in that way. What are you feeling when you do this thing that you dislike?

If your behavior is caused by a negative emotion, what is the root of that emotion? Is it a meaning you have given to something that has been done to you? Is it something that you have learned from the people around you or from your life experience? Changing the behavior won't change the emotion. You need to change the emotion itself and to do that you need to change the meaning that you give to it.

If it's a belief that is causing the behavior, then once again, you need to look back at the cause of the belief. All of our beliefs and all of our emotions are rooted in *something*, whether it is biological, cognitive or social – and it's usually all three. Human complexity can make it difficult to work back to the reason, and sometimes there is no one, single reason.

Let me give you an example. Someone rudely pushes past you on the street, and then walks off without apologizing. How do you react?

I'd say that the most common answer I receive to this one is "angry". Aggressive and upset also come up a lot, but anger is the most common. I also get told that this is a perfectly normal response, surely? And that this being the case, why is it a bad thing, and why would you want to change it?

Yes, to be fair, it is a perfectly natural human response, but it's not necessarily helpful to you. Dumping a load of hormones in your system while you stress about this person's actions might do damage to your own health, but it's doing nothing to him. Not only do you get the annoyance of having been pushed, you get a system full of excess levels of cortisol.

The physiological response of anger is a product of your beliefs and attitudes. Why has this affected you strongly enough to make you react in this way? Perhaps when you were younger, your dad told you that allowing people to push you around makes you less of a man. The belief that you are reacting to, then, is that this person's behavior has challenged your own concept of yourself. The emotional response of anger is generated by this social conditioning. These combine to give you an attitude that someone pushing past you is a threat or a challenge to your status, and that it should make you angry. Any behaviors that follow will come from that attitude. If you gave the aggressive answer, your behavior might even be to run after him and challenge him. You could change this behavior – maybe by reminding yourself that fighting in the middle of the street is going to get you into as much trouble as the other guy – but that would not change the attitude, the belief or the emotion.

Those who said that they were upset are also reading something into the situation – remember, we read something into every situation. Perhaps you are a quiet, shy person who feels that others don't respect you. Your cognitive processes tell you that this means that people ignore and overlook you. Your social conditioning has reinforced this, maybe because you have always been the quiet one in the family, or in meetings at work, and your voice doesn't get heard as much as the voices of more forceful people. The emotional response of being upset comes from those thought processes, which have just been reinforced by the person pushing you. The belief is that you are a person who is always being disrespected by people. The attitude then is that you are a quiet person who will always let other people walk over you, and the behavior you get will be a by-product of that.

The issue with both of these reactions is that you have made it *personal*. You've taken this as a personal threat or insult, and reacted accordingly, according to your biopsychosocial programming.

Ok, now think about this. What if the guy who pushed you was late for a job interview, or had just found out that his father had been taken into hospital, or his wife had gone into labor? You have taken his actions personally – he may not even have noticed you!

Perhaps he was just rude. Do you care? If he had no manners, are you going to let him ruin your day, or even a few minutes of it?

What would I do? I'd probably think "How rude!" and then walk on. And seconds later it would be out of my head completely. I don't waste time on thinking about things that annoy me, that have already happened, and that I can't do anything about. I also don't waste time worrying about other people's bad behavior, unless it has some ongoing impact on my life. I certainly don't let their behavior affect mine.

This, by the way, is the result of putting my own methods into practice. At one time, I took everything personally, and all my behaviors were the result of my beliefs that anything bad that happened to me was a personal attack, and my emotional responses to my conditioning. I promise you, it's a lot more relaxing to have the programming in your head that makes your behavior work for rather than against you!

It's a sad fact of life that things will always happen that you don't like, from small unpleasant situations like the one above, right on up. Take the emotional, personal meaning out of a situation and you will get a different response. Take the unhelpful belief out of the situation and you will get a better response. Your attitude to the things that happen to and around you will change, and your behaviors will change along with that.

Think again about the model that we looked at earlier, and how it all links together:

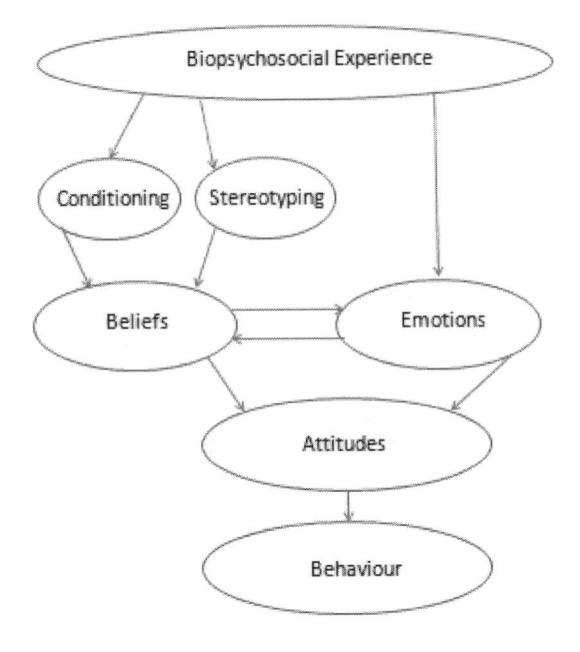

```
                    Biopsychosocial Experience
                   /       |        |        \
        Conditioning   Stereotyping  |
              \         /            |
               Beliefs  ⇄       Emotions
                    \           /
                      Attitudes
                          |
                      Behaviour
```

The area that you are working with is right at the top. You have looked at how your biology, your thought processes and your social experience work, and you've looked at some ways in which you can make them work together. You've also looked at how your conditioning and stereotyping has taken place over the course of your life, and some ways to change that. You have considered the impact on your beliefs and your feelings, the influence that these will have on your attitudes and therefore your behaviors. You understand that the power to do what you want to do lies in your mind, and that your mind can hinder or support you , depending on how you program it, and you have some tools to work with. You're now ready to start to put it all together.

In the next chapter, you will work on your own personal action plan.

19 ACTION PLAN

Having reached the end of the book, you should now have a much clearer understanding of why everything really is all in your mind – and how your genetics, the way that you think and your experience to date has combined to make you the person that you are today. The last stage, then, is to put it all together, and to begin to apply it to your own life and your own circumstances. I have found that the best way to do this is to put together an action plan, which allows you to look back to understand why you are as you are, and to look forward to take yourself where you want to be.

What we will do now is work through the steps in your own personal action plan to bring about the changes that you want in your life. Take your time with this – there is no rush. You have built yourself up through many years of experience, it is worthwhile to spend as much time as you need working through the steps. Don't put yourself under pressure to perform instantly. Working through your plan, discovering new things that you are capable of and new horizons to explore, should be exciting. I want you to enjoy the experience of planning the person that you can be, and the future that you can have.

Before you start working through the plan, I would suggest that you make sure you pick a time when you are as relaxed as you can be. Make sure that you won't be disturbed, as you will need to know that you have the peace and quiet that you really need to be able to think about these fundamental things affecting your life. Take a pen and paper with you, as you will need to write some things down.

Planning, understanding and control are all vital steps on the path to achieving any goal or desire. Commitment and belief are also critical, and to have these things, you need to have a clear vision of where you want to go. The time that you spend up-front working through your plan will pay huge dividends in the future.

Bear in mind that you are taking a big step here, one that many people will never take. You are taking specific action to make changes in your life.

STEP 1 – Reviewing your self-concept

Look back over the list of characteristics that you wrote down in Chapter 1. In light of what you have learned since, which of these do you still consider to be an accurate representation of yourself?

Do you think that any of the items on the list are ideas that you have about yourself, based on a past experience or your own beliefs about how other people view you? When looked at in that light, do you think that they are all correct, or have you changed your mind about some of these things? If so, which ones, and why? Rewrite your list again, noticing any things that have changed.

STEP 2 – Understanding your self-concept

Think about the items on your list that have changed. What has shifted in your beliefs for you to realize that this was not a correct way of seeing yourself? What did it take to make you believe that in the first instance? Be aware of what measures you see as a verification of the truth – an event in your life, a reoccurrence of events, things that people said to you. It's very important that you recognize the factors that make something believable to you; both so that you can be aware of the things that life events or people can force you to take on board, and so that you are aware of what it will take to convince you that you really have made a change.

STEP 3 – Refining your self-concept

Make yourself a new list, with three columns. One will represent the things that you like about yourself, and want to build upon. One will represent things that you would to have, do or be, which you don't feel are currently part of your life at the moment. One will represent traits or things in your life which don't make you happy, and which you would like to change.

Call these columns anything that appeals to you, which really makes you feel what you are trying to capture in them. You could call them "More Me", "New Me" and "Not Me", for example. It doesn't actually matter what name you use. This is your list, and you can use whatever works for you. All you need to understand is that we all have some things that we do have but would like to develop more, some things that we don't have but feel that we need, and some things that we do have and wish we didn't! For example, you might list "Patience" in column one, "Confidence" in column 2, and "Self-Doubt" in column three.

STEP 4 – Reviewing your goals

Read back over the goals that you wrote down in chapter 4. Select the ones that you are most passionate about, and write these down in a new list. When you have done this, look back over the new list and consider the following:

What does each goal mean to you? What do you think that it would bring into your life that you don't have now? Take the time to really feel the meaning of each goal.

What do you need to work on if you are going to achieve your goal? Do you need some of the traits that you listed in columns 1 and 2 above? Do you need to get rid of some of the things that you wrote down in column 3?

STEP 5 – Assessing your skills

Go back to the list of skills that you wrote down in Chapter 1. Make another set of two columns on your new sheet. In the first one, write these down again. Now, look back at the goals that you have set for yourself. Do you have all of the skills and knowledge that you think you will need to achieve them, or do you need more? In the second column of your table, write down anything that you think you will need to learn to achieve your goals. Take some time to consider these. What could you do to achieve them? Call your lists something like "Skills I Have" and "Skills I Need".

STEP 6 – Challenging your beliefs

You now have three new sets of information. You have an assessment of your traits – those that you have that are good, those that you would like to have, and those that you have that are unhelpful. You have a list of goals. You have a list of the skills that you have, and the skills that you feel that you need to develop.

Taken altogether, these lists give you a pretty good overview of where you feel you are at present, both in terms of what is currently in your life, and the things that you want to be there. However, they are just that – an overview. Having read this book all the way through, you will understand that what is here on this list is colored by your social experience, your genetic make-up, and your way of thinking.

What I would like you to do now is to consider this information as a whole, and challenge the accuracy of it. What kind of a picture does it give you of the person that you are? Do you feel that it is an accurate representation of yourself?

You have already started to think, in the earlier steps, about the things that you wrote down about your traits, and why you believe them. Now, instead of just looking at single traits, you can look at yourself as a whole. You start to do this by looking at each trait individually, and as you do this you will start to build up a picture of the things that have influenced your development, and made you who you are today.

For example, if you have written in the traits that you do not like that you are a negative person, is this something that's natural, or is it learned? Remember conditioning. Have you always been negative, or have circumstances in life made you react in that way? Has classical conditioning taught you to associate certain things with bad results? If you are shy, or aggressive, is this something that is spontaneous, or has operant conditioning taught you that this is the best way to get something that you want, or to stop something happening that you don't want? Is your reaction conscious or subconscious? Can you understand what has made you this way, and think of a way to behave that would give you a more positive result?

Now think back to stereotyping. What you are looking at is effectively the information that you hold in the schema about yourself. That does not mean it's totally accurate. You understand now that you have built up this information over the course of a lifetime. Can you think back to certain events in your life that gave you these impressions of yourself? If you have written down that you are weak-willed, or incompetent, or anything else negative, what put that information in your mind? Think back to step 2 – what would it take to change it, and to convince yourself of the change?

Are you holding any negative thoughts in your head from your childhood environment – such as thinking that because you didn't excel at school you can't be intelligent, or because you came from a poor background you can't be rich? You need to challenge any and all of the beliefs that you feel restrict your growth. Remember, these things shaped you, but they do not define you. You define yourself.

STEP 7 – Trying on your goal

Start with one of your goals. Pick the one that means the most to you – the person that you really want to be, the thing that you really want to achieve. The process will be the same for every goal, but the first time you do this, it helps if you choose the goal that you feel really passionate about.

Now start to think about how your traits and skills line up to this goal. What you are aiming to do is to understand your beliefs around achieving it, the reasons why you think you could do it and the reasons why you might think that you cannot. You have already challenged the beliefs which might previously have held you back. Now start looking at those things that are left, in the areas of skills and knowledge, that are lacking for this particular goal. What do you think now about your ability to achieve it? Can you understand the things that you already have that will help you to get there, and can you feel confident that you can obtain those that you will need?

Now, take a few minutes to consider what emotions you are feeling when you think about your goal. Do you feel excited? Confident? Nervous? Does it feel totally congruent for you, or is there something about it that makes you uneasy? If so, try to think what that is. Remember, our goals are not always our own. If you understand the steps that you need to take in order to reach your goal, and it really is meeting your own personal desire, you should feel positive emotions around it. Make sure that you are not spending your time working towards something that somebody else wanted for you.

STEP 8 – Building your new identity

Okay, this is the big step. You've done the basics of trying out your new identity. Now you are going to wear it.

Stand up and take a few deep breaths, until you feel really calm and focused. Now you are going to start to build up the feeling of being what or who you want to be.

Consider that person, the new you. What traits and skills would you have? Imagine that the new you is standing right in front of you, ready for you to build on all of the things that you want for yourself. Now, you are going to think about people whom you admire who already have those things, and borrow them.

If you need confidence, think of someone that you consider to be really confident, and imagine how that confidence would feel on you. If you want to be calm, or patient, or competent, do the same. If you need a certain skill, think of someone who excels in that field, and imagine how it would feel to have their knowledge. It doesn't matter how many things you need, I promise you that someone out there has them, and that you can model them.

Once you are happy that you have all of the things that you need, take a deep breath, and step forward into that space where you have built the new you, with all the skills and traits that you need to achieve your goal. How do you feel?

You need to experience this on all levels. How do you feel physically? What are your emotions? How do you think? What do you see ahead of you? Who are the people around you? What exciting things do you have in your life?

Stay there until you can really experience what it is like to be this new you. When you are happy that you have really experienced what life would be like after these changes, take a deep breath, and touch your fingers to your arm, or squeeze your fists together, to anchor that experience. Then, in your own time, you can step out of that space.

This is state change. Once you have done this, it's always there and accessible to you. Whenever you need to, you will be able to repeat your anchoring gesture, take a deep breath, and bring back the experience. It's yours.

Whenever things are bad, or you are feeling despondent, do this, and remind yourself how you felt. When you wake up feeling miserable, repeat that you are happy, or successful, or confident, or even just that it's going to be a good day, and you will capture some of that feeling back.

STEP 9 – Working on the negative feelings

Now that you have experienced how simply your mind can change your state, you can consider two other things. The first is your negative emotions. Give the choice of feeling as you did earlier, or feeling angry, or hurt, or dissatisfied, which will you choose? Secondly, you now have something to hold up against your secondary gain. Would feeling like that outweigh any secondary gain that you are achieving from your current situation? If not, you have the wrong goal!

It's easy to slip into negativity when you cannot see any way out of it. Now you have not only seen a way out, you have felt and experienced it – and you also have the mental tools to ensure that you will never lose all hope or all control. You will find that this makes a huge difference to the way that you experience life.

STEP 10 – Go out there and do it!

20 CONCLUSION

And here we are, at the end of the book. Congratulations for making the commitment to keep reading to the end. You have already done more than many people ever do, in starting to bring about change in your life.

I hope that you can now understand why it is so critical to take charge of your mind: to understand how it works and why, the ways in which it is programmed, and the methods that you can use to control it. I also hope that you are feeling a sense of excitement, and a heightened ability to control your own destiny; and that you will bring this and your new knowledge together to help you focus on and achieve your goals.

If I had to name my deepest hope for this book, it is that it will allow people to understand that nobody has to spend the remainder of the life as a victim of their past. We all have the ability to make a choice: to live with what we have been given, or to make the decision to take our own path, follow our own dreams, and refuse to let the things we have learned previously hold us back. This is something that many people sadly never grasp. I think the main reason for this is often that either they do not know where to start, or that they do not have the tools to allow them to do it. This book offers both the tools and the starting point. The rest is up to you.

Too many people feel that they are confined by the past, and I want you to really believe that this does not have to be the case. Having had an easy start in life is obviously an advantage, but it's nothing more. You have the power, if you are prepared to put in the time, effort and commitment that it takes, to give your mind all the processes and ways of functioning that it needs to let you achieve your goals. The most important things are not intelligence, or education, or upbringing. The most important things are commitment and self-belief.

You should now have a good understanding of why things that happened in your past life – ranging from simple comments by another person to traumatic events – continue to affect you in the present. You have also been given a toolkit which will allow you to step in and interrupt your mind when it is giving a negative response, and to replace that response with something more positive. Combine those with an absolute determination to achieve your goal, and patience with and faith in yourself, and you will see absolutely amazing changes begin to happen in your life.

I am not telling you that this will happen overnight. You are working against a lifetime of programming, strengthened by repetition over the years. However, I have found that, for most people, the ability just to understand why they feel, think and react as they do brings about an immediate change. You no longer need to take whatever your mind chooses to hand out to you. You can be in charge.

Learn to recognize the signs that you are unhappy with something, and to immediately challenge it and make an intervention. These responses will become automatic, as your previous responses did. After a time, you will immediately sense when something does not feel right, and step in to make a different choice or response.

Many people tell me that they began to see immediate small changes after they started to put the principles in this book into practice. These changes impact the whole biopsychosocial field. Physical changes in the body and the mind lead to an increased feeling of well-being. Changes in thought processes lead to the ability to reframe meanings in a more beneficial way. Changes in social interactions lead to better relationships and increased confidence. The whole, put together, allows you to feel more at peace with yourself, and to have more faith in your own ability to deal with life with all its challenges.

You also now have the ability and understanding to address these things directly. You know how to make physiological changes by amending your body posture and actions. You know how to make cognitive changes by challenging negative thoughts and interpretations of meaning, and by always asking questions like "How Could I…?" You know how to get the most benefit from your social relationships, by seeking to understand the meanings that you are taking from other people, understanding that they have rules and meaning interpretations too, and understanding that you have the ability to challenge and reject anything that is imposed on you with which you do not agree.

One of the saddest things I see is the number of people who suppress their own dreams and goals, purely because they cannot see how to attain them. Unfortunately, most of us are not encouraged to aspire. Instead, we are told to think small, play safe, and conform to the rules of the majority. Parents and teachers generally do not teach you how to do things differently, because they are not taught this themselves. Unfortunately, if you spend your whole life playing safe and doing what is expected of you by those around you and by society, you will never get to truly fulfill your own desires.

You can imagine what effect this has, if it is the example that we see around us, day in and day out. Many of the people around you may not understand what you are trying to do, or take your aspirations seriously. This does not mean that you are being unrealistic (and if you've worked through this book, you will know for yourself whether your goals are realistic or not). It simply means that you have chosen to create your own reality, in the way that you want it to be, rather than just to accept the reality that you have been given.

Standing out from the crowd takes a degree of courage. However, think about it this way. Would you prefer to stay in the shadows and accept things as they are now, or take the steps that you must to move out into the future that you want? Can you accept that change will always have its own challenges, but that the motivation outweighs the pain? Can you stay true to your new beliefs, in the face of challenge and skepticism? It takes a special kind of person to be able to do this. I truly believe that everyone has the ability to be a special kind of person.

Once you have mastered these principles for yourself, you will also be able to help those around you to take control of their own minds and reach out for their goals. Of course, not everyone will be ready and willing to make changes. Never try to impose your own beliefs on people, or try to force them to make changes: it will not work, and it will leave you demoralized. However, you will be amazed, as I was, at the number of people who begin to ask your advice once they see the changes in you. Never underestimate the pleasure that you can get from helping others. Share your experience and you will be rewarded many times over.

I would recommend that you read this book periodically, and most specifically when you are feeling a lack of confidence or motivation. I would also keep it to hand, and refer back to specific sections, whenever you feel the need of some extra support in that area.

Also, remember that you are not limited to whichever dream or goal you named as your primary one. You can work through the action plan in the last chapter with any number of goals and aspirations. Your only limit is your imagination, and the skills and knowledge that you need around you, and the mental and emotional commitment which you need to make to each goal. One goal at a time seems to work best for most people. When you start seeing improvement in that area, and are satisfied that you are on track to get your result, you can move on to the next.

You will find, if you carry on following the principles

of the book, that problems become easier to handle, and that challenges are no longer so daunting. Of course, this is not due to the nature of the problems or challenges – it is due to the nature of you. The mind is like any muscle; it needs exercise. The more you exercise it, the more adept it will become. If you have let your brain sit on tickover for years, don't fall into the trap of thinking that it will not learn any more. You understand now that brain plasticity will ensure that your brain makes the connections it needs, once you start to consistently use it. Don't undersell yourself based on past experience. You are never too old or too out of practice to learn.

Far too many people lead lives full of misery and sadness, feeling that they have missed out on things that they should have had, and that they have been cheated out of their dreams. I urge you not to be one of them. Use this book as the start of a greater journey in life, one in which you have fun, and challenges, and the satisfaction of knowing that you are working towards having the things around you that you truly want. It does not matter what these are – they are individual to each person. It doesn't matter whether what you want is a thriving business, good relationships, a fulfilling career or greater financial security – or simply a feeling of love and satisfaction towards yourself. What matters is that the things which you are working towards are important to *you*.

I will close, then, by reminding you that your happiness is valuable. Life is long, and it should be enjoyable. I believe that every human being has the right to live a fulfilling, satisfying life. I also believe that happiness, contentment and confidence are all habits, which can be built like any other habit, and which will become second nature after a time. The more confident, happy and fulfilled you are, the more you will feel able to aim for your dreams. Also, you will find that the happier you are, the happier the people around you become. Like many things in life, this is a circle, and it works from its own momentum. You have the ability to set the ball rolling. All you need to do now is to take the first step.

ABOUT THE AUTHOR

Lindsey Sharratt holds an Honours degree in Psychology. She plans to complete a research PhD in Cognitive Psychology, specializing in her fields of interest: autobiographical memory, working self and emotion. Lindsey is also committed to making psychology more accessible to everyone, and to promoting an understanding of self-concept development to a wider audience. In addition to her academic work, she teaches, writes and speaks around self-concept issues and interventions.

www.lindseysharratt.com

https://www.facebook.com/lindsey.sharratt.self.concept.specialist
https://www.facebook.com/LindseySharratt.ItsAllInYourMind
https://www.linkedin.com/in/lindseysharrattselfconcept
https://twitter.com/LindseySharratt

Printed in Great Britain
by Amazon